BIG FAT FOOD FRAUD

Confessions of a Health-Food Hustler

Jeff Scot Philips

Regan Arts.

New York

Regan Arts.

65 Bleecker Street
New York, NY 10012

First Regan Arts hardcover edition, October 2016

Library of Congress Control Number: 2016939708

ISBN 978-1-942872-87-0

Names and identifying details of some of the people portrayed in this book have been changed.

Interior design by Nancy Singer
Cover design by Richard Ljoenes

Images page 217 courtesy of *(left)* Valentyn Volkov © 123RF.com and *(right)* Anna Liebiedieva © 123RF.com; page 219 *(left)* leeavison © 123RF.com and *(right)* Victoria Ryabinina © 123RF.com.

Printed in the United States of America

10 9 8 7 6 5 4 3 2 1

CONTENTS

INTRODUCTION

I'M MAKING YOU FAT

I control what you eat, I control how much of it and how often. I dictate how your doctor advises you, as well as what your dietitian and personal trainer recommend to you. I plant the health articles you read in your newspaper, and the messages you hear when you watch the news or your favorite daytime doctor personality.

I'm even manipulating the ingredients in that healthy meal you bought at your gym and the label you read to make sure it is good for you; after all, everything you know about reading food labels, I taught you. Everything you *think* you know about nutrition and weight loss comes from me.

My name is Jeff Scot Philips. I'm the founder and CEO of a health-food manufacturer that prepares meals for national gym franchises, medical weight loss facilities, grocery stores, and fitness celebrities all across the United States. In fact, if you've ever eaten a healthy prepackaged meal (think Lean Cuisine, but tastier) you might have eaten my food and not known it.

You would be horrified if you knew all the ways I can manipulate my ingredients and food labels. For example, did you know that according to the United States Department of Agriculture, salmon isn't a lean, healthy food because of its high fat content? So guess what companies like mine do to get around this: we add refined sugars, usually in the form of pastas and bread, to increase the total calories while keeping the grams of fat the same, which legally makes salmon a lean, healthy meal.

And if you think that's deceptive and irresponsible, you probably won't want to read the next sentence.

When our food labels say "No HFCS (high-fructose corn-syrup)," that doesn't mean there's no HFCS (*wink*). Once we've added sugar to make our seafood healthy, the USDA doesn't care what we do with it next—we don't even have to mention any of the ingredients! We can take a crab cake and pump it full of gluten and HFCS, and we don't have to mention either one on the nutrition label. Could people with allergies to gluten get sick? You bet! But these ingredients are very cheap for us, and if you, the health-conscious consumer, don't know that they're in there you'll buy more, and we'll profit more!

As a food manufacturer I'm totally out of control, I don't answer to anyone, and I manipulate whatever I have to, to sell product. But even *that* isn't the truly scary part. This is:

I'm the one educating you on health.

The reason baby boomers think egg yolks are high in cholesterol and lead to increased chances of heart attack is thanks to John Harvey Kellogg, founder of Kellogg's Corn Flakes, who claimed that in an ad campaign. If you've ever heard that chocolate has health benefits, that's because the Mars, Incorporated (Snickers, M&M's, Twix, Milky Way) funded the research on it. Did you know that calories were created—not discovered—by two guys named Merrill and Watt in 1955? And when Elisabeth Hasselbeck sparked the gluten paranoia in 2009, she empowered food companies like mine to slap a gluten-free label on chips and cookies that people started buying more than ever, which lead to a rapid increase of obesity in America.

I pay big-name fitness celebrities to endorse my food, I publically intimidate politicians to push my competitors out, I travel the country sleeping with personal trainers so that they'll promote my meals, and when my on-site USDA agent wouldn't approve my questionable nutrition labels I had to bribe him, though not with money; I did it by bringing a Miss America contestant friend of mine to spend the afternoon with him. My labels got approved the next day.

Business is good. But the kicker is: all of this corporate corruption, ingredient deviancy, and food label fraud keeps me up at night. I don't want to do this to people's food. I'm not happy about making people fatter and lying to their face about it.

But, as you'll see, I can't stop either.

PART 1

PART 1

BRIBING THE HEALTH INSPECTOR

My head was in the back of a hot, dust-filled commercial oven, and there was a man tugging on my shirt and screaming at me at the top of his lungs. My eyes were watering so bad I could barely see, and every time I tried to breathe, my lungs filled with soot and I started coughing violently. The oven had just finished auto-cleaning and I was scraping out the burned ashes to make it look brand-new.

The man yelling at me was the owner of the kitchen space I was renting—we'll call him Christopher—and he had a lot of money to lose if we failed the inspection, so he kept screaming, "Hurry the fuck up! Come on. Come on. Come on!" Every thirty seconds, he stopped shouting at me only long enough to direct the chefs, who were running in and out of the room with their arms full of kitchen equipment. They were transporting all of our abused cooking utensils across the hall to be locked in the office and then replaced with our "display utensils," the equipment we never used (health code violation 3.2-5110). We were down to twenty minutes before the health inspector would arrive, which meant we had fifteen minutes to get the place looking like a showroom kitchen and to get the hell out of there.

I was a virgin in the food service industry. I hadn't worked in a real kitchen before; I hadn't even done any research before starting my healthy meal delivery company. I had no clue what the health codes were, other than the common sense ones, like always washing my hands and keeping food off the floor. Christopher, however, owned numerous properties, so he knew that we were in violation of various health code laws, and if he wanted to keep us as tenants, we had to cover up those violations to avoid getting shut down.

I guess I should have known that everyone handling food was required to be trained in food safety, which they weren't (health code violation 5-421-70 [12]), or that the staff needed an operational bathroom, which they didn't have (health code violation 5-421-2240), or that we were supposed to have three side-by-side sinks—one for washing, one for rinsing, and one for sanitizing (health code violation 3.2-5106). Had I done my research, I would have known that we were required to have an industrial strength dishwasher, properly elevated food storage units, and grease traps for the sinks—none of which we had (health code violations . . . well, you get the idea). Rather than correcting all these things at the last minute, Christopher thought it would be easier—i.e., cheaper—to make it look as if the space wasn't being used as a commercial kitchen at all, which would change the rules that applied to us. And, thanks to the health department, it was very easy for us to do this.

Health inspectors schedule their visits weeks in advance (which is nowhere near as lazy as the USDA's approach, which is to review detailed reports of our operations—that *we* create!). Even better for us, they actually let the kitchen owner choose the time and date of the appointment, which gave us plenty of time to create a pristine kitchen. So my crew and I spent the forty-eight hours leading up to the inspection scrubbing countertops, painting the walls, bleaching the refrigerators, Krud-Kutting the mountains of soot caked at the bottom of the ovens, steaming the floors, pouring gallons of grease into emptied plastic containers to be tossed into our neighbor's trash can, and hiding all the equipment we actually used to prepare food.

Not only were we breaking just about every health code there was, but we were also going to blatantly lie about it to the inspector. But under the pressure of the moment, all I knew was that I didn't want to lose my newly formed company, so I just kept my mouth shut and followed Christopher's lead.

With thirty seconds to spare, we had the kitchen looking like the set of a daytime cooking show, and as I heard the inspector walking up the stairs to the kitchen door, I yanked the chefs into the crowded office with me and pulled the door shut, locking us in.

There was no question that the health inspector would give us a passing grade now. On a typical day, you'd see people scrambling all over the place, handling food nonstop from five a.m. to nine p.m. Although we were averaging twelve hundred meals per day, there were no traces of food in any of the five refrigerators; the ovens and stove tops looked as though they'd never been turned on; you could see your reflection on the sparkling pots and pans that were sitting on top of the Windex-coated countertops; and, most convincing of all, there were zero cooks in sight.

I was standing wedged between our kitchen equipment and the chefs with my ear to the door, listening as Christopher lied his way through the inspection. "Oh, those? We just use those for, uh, our cooking classes." . . . "No, we don't charge for the food itself, only for the education." . . . "Of course! I plan to have the bathroom fully functional by the end of the week." . . . "Well no, *I* don't handle the food." . . . "The guy who's renting the space? He couldn't be here today." . . . "No problem, whatever we need to do." . . . "OK, how much?"

After fifteen or twenty minutes of Christopher's smoke blowing, I heard the kitchen door slam, followed by silence. I waited a few extra minutes, then opened the door and peeked out. On the counter sat a certificate noting that we had passed our inspection. Beside the certificate was an informal invoice from Christopher for five-hundred bucks with a small handwritten note at the bottom: "Your half."

A couple of hours later, it was dark out and the chefs had all gone home for the night. I was wheeling the last tray rack from the office back into the kitchen, when I heard what sounded like a faint knock at the door.

Tap-tap-tap.

I stopped moving.

Tap-tap-tap.

I tried swallowing the golf ball in my throat. I grabbed Christopher's invoice off the table, crumpled the evidence, and threw it into the trash.

Tap-tap-tap. Tap-tap-tap.

I opened the door to see this gorgeous middle-aged woman in a business suit eyeballing me.

I swung the door all the way out, making enough room for her to step through.

"Hi, what can I do for you?" I asked.

After giving the kitchen a brief once-over, then turning back to me, she said, "I'm guessing you're Jeff."

I hesitated, wondering how she knew my name. "Yeah, I'm Jeff. Is there something I can help you with?"

"I understand your kitchen had a health inspection today."

"Yes, it did. We passed with flying colors," I pointed behind her. "The certificate's right over there on the wall."

Without bothering to look, she continued, "I have a few questions for you. Let's speak in your office." She signaled for me to lead the way.

She locked the door behind her, rejected the chair I offered, and asked, "How long have you been in business?"

I shrugged, "Just a couple of months."

"And I understand Christopher is the one who met with your health inspector, not you."

"Yeah," I confirmed, "it's his property. I'm just renting the space, ya know."

"But you own the company that employs the people who handle the food, correct?"

Wondering whether I was trapping myself, I tried playing innocent, "Yeah, that's right. Was I supposed to meet with the inspector too?"

Then she threw a complete curveball: "Have you ever eaten at [hidden name], the little mom-and-pop Italian restaurant around the corner?"

Bewildered, I affirmed, "Uh, sure, plenty of times."

"Do you like the food?"

"Yeah, the food's good but—look, I'm sorry for being blunt, but what are you getting at? Did something go wrong with our inspection today?"

"I'm glad you prefer bluntness, because that place hasn't come close to passing inspection on its best day, and it would have been shut down years ago if the owner hadn't worked out a deal with me."

"OK. What kind of deal? Who are you?"

She finally broke her stern demeanor with a tiny smile, "The owner of that place is more concerned about who my husband is, because he knows if my husband were to find out how he runs his restaurant, it wouldn't be open the next morning—which is why he worked out a deal with me. The deal is that I'll keep my husband away from his kitchen. Would you like me to keep my husband away from your kitchen too?"

Finally grasping the big picture, I pressed back, "That's interesting, but I don't know who your husband is, and, like I said, we passed our inspection, so there's nothing to make a deal about."

She stepped right up to me, bringing her face only a few inches away from mine, "What if my husband were to show up tomorrow or the next day while your employees are in here, cooking; will it still be up to code then?"

Her smile faded away when I said, "Look, I don't know who your husband works for, but Christopher already took care of our health inspector, so he may want to check—"

Without warning, she smacked her hand into my crotch, sending a shockwave up through my stomach, then clamped down with her fingers and repeated her offer, "You're running a commercial food business out of a *non*commercial kitchen." She spouted off a quick list of code violations, "no repackaged container labels: 5-421-480; improper utensil storage: 5-421-550 produce sitting next to packaged meals: 5-421-470 . . . Now, do you want me to keep my husband away from your kitchen or not?"

I coughed out a response, "Ehhh, OK." I gripped her forearm, but it only made her squeeze harder.

Calmly, she asked again, "So you want to work out a deal, then?"

"Fine—that's fine. Wha-whatever w-we need to, eh, to do!"

She cracked her little smile again, "Good," then loosened her grip.

Defeated, I asked, "So, do I need to work out a regular payment to you . . . or how does this work?"

"That's right." Her clamping turned to fondling. "Once a month, right here."

"Working out a deal with me isn't so bad," she assured me, as I started to get hard. Then she locked my hair between her fingers, pulled me in toward her. I was a little gray on which one of us was breaking what law, but at that moment, I didn't really give a shit.

When she left twenty minutes later, I still had no idea of who the hell she or her husband were, but I knew I had just been hazed into something I didn't know how to get out of. I dubbed her the Extortion Cougar.

This was the beginning of my journey into the food and weight-loss industry and when I first learned about the corruption, manipulation, and bribes. If someone had told me that in three years the company I would start in my little condo kitchen would be producing and shipping food for other health companies all across the country, or that I would be working with fitness gurus, investors, government agencies, and the media to push shitty food on unsuspecting American consumers, I would have said, "You're fucking crazy." But this was about to become my new world.

1

HOW TO LOSE SEVEN POUNDS IN SEVEN DAYS

"How many times do we have to go through this, Libby? Reese's Peanut Butter Cups aren't on your diet plan."

"That's why I come to you," she said, "so I can work off the calories."

"You know it doesn't work like that, and besides—*hey!*" I shouted to the man at the far end of the row of treadmills. "Could you please not do that?" Jed knew better than to run backward on the treadmill. Just the other week, he and I both watched the gym's resident CrossFit enthusiast, Adam, sprinting backward on the very same machine, when he lost his balance and shot off the back, tripped over his own foot, and was left lying facedown in the middle of the gym. "Jed, you know that's asking for trouble, man," I said, but he waved me off and kept running.

I turned back to my client, who was manually pushing her treadmill with the power off—a *far* more taxing exercise than it would be with the power on. "Libby, I'm looking through your diet log and—come on, keep up the pace—and I'm not seeing a single vegetable in here . . . did you forget to document them?"

"No," she said with a guilty face. "Manny told me I didn't have to eat them."

Libby, the gym's black sheep, was in her midsixties and at five-five she was a full foot shorter than me, but carried about two hundred twenty-five pounds on a frame intended for about one-eighty. You would think she'd be eager to follow my dietary instructions, but instead her favorite pastime was hanging around my gym all day, defying everything I said and generally causing mischief.

"Libby, we both know Manny wouldn't tell you that."

"OK, fine, so I didn't eat any this week; big deal."

"I'm getting tired of going over this. Without veggies, you're going to have inflammation, and you're never going to lose those last forty-five pounds if you don't—*Hey, not so fast, Karen!*"

Out of the corner of my eye, I saw another client sneaking toward the front door. "I need your food diary from last week before you leave, and I better not see any you-know-what in there." She pulled a notebook from her gym bag and sulked as she made her way over to me.

I was used to coming off as the bad guy. If I was going to keep my gym's reputation as the best in Roanoke City, I needed all my clients to be getting results, which meant I couldn't give them an inch. I grabbed her notebook and flipped through a couple of pages.

"Do you guys just enjoy wasting money?" I asked her and Libby. "Seriously, what are you paying me for if you're not going to listen to me?"

"I'm sorry," they said in unison. There was an incessant ringing from the phone at the front desk that was getting on my nerves.

"It's just so hard," Karen continued. "Sometimes I get busy at work and have to settle for snack food. . . . I'm trying to do better, though."

"I hear ya, Karen, but four months now? Something's gotta change."

"Look, I want to see you at my nutrition workshop next Saturday;

we'll talk more about this—" The phone was still ringing. "*Hey, guys!*" I shouted to the trainers loitering around the smoothie bar arguing loudly about whether Barack would beat Hillary in the upcoming primaries. "Can someone answer that please?"

"I've gotta run, Jeff," Karen said. "I'm going to be late for work, but I'll see you next Saturday."

"Sounds good, Karen. Libby, keep your knees up." Libby was barely moving on the treadmill.

"But it hurts," she whined. "I think I need to sit down for a few minutes."

"You can sit down during the twenty-three hours you're not with me; but for the next fifteen minutes, I need you to sta—"

"*Hey, Jeff!*" my newest trainer, Tiffany, shouted across the gym, "It's Natalie from Channel Ten; she wants to know whether she can swing by and record a quick segment for tomorrow's show."

Libby whispered loudly into my ear, "I can't believe you hired a lesbian trainer."

"I'm not in the mood for your homophobic nonsense today," I said to Libby. "Just stay focused on what you're doing, please."

Tiffany shouted again, "What should I tell her?"

There was a loud thud and I turned to see Jed lying facedown in the middle of the gym. I could tell by the red-faced smile he was giving me that his pride had been hurt more than anything.

"Tiffany, tell her we'll have to call them back—go help Jed please; make sure he's OK."

"She's not going to give him mouth-to-mouth; you know they find guys repulsive," Libby whispered as Tiffany and two other trainers zoomed toward Jed.

"First of all, nobody does mouth-to-mouth anymore," I said to Libby, "but, just in case—given that you're straight—if Jed needs CPR, do you want to be on deck for mouth-to-mouth?" She scrunched up her face.

"He's all right!" Tiffany shouted from the opposite corner of the gym, as the three of them helped Jed to his feet.

I felt a tap on my shoulder and turned to see who it was. "Hey, Jeff, sorry to interrupt," another of my longtime clients, Joy, said, "but I just had to swing by and show you this note my doctor wrote for you."

Dear Mr. Philips,

I want to thank you for your extensive work in our collaborated efforts with Joy. Since working with you, she has shown remarkable progress, and I'm happy to inform you that her type 2 diabetes has been presently cured.

I gave Joy a giant hug. "I knew you could do it! I'm so proud of you!" Joy was the pickiest eater I'd ever met, so it was quite the uphill battle getting her diet on track. We had daily check-in calls; I helped overhaul her entire kitchen pantry; and I spent hours with her husband and children to teach them how important it was to be supportive of her health.

"Can you believe it?" she said, glassy-eyed. "No more needles! Many thanks for harassing me twenty-four-seven."

"Joy, you know I'm always willing to harass you! Hey, speaking of harassing, you're going to be at the workshop next weekend, right? It's on managing food cravings and, most importantly for you, how to maintain results."

"Already reserved my seat!"

"Perfect! Oh, and don't forget I need to see you for a ten-minute pop-in two weeks from now so we can get your measurements; we still need to keep a close eye on your blood pressure, so before you head out, swing by the front desk and book a time slot."

I turned back to Libby. "That reminds me, you know I'm going to the Arnold Classic this weekend, but I've set you up to work out with Tiffany, and she's going to take great care of you."

"I can't work out with a gay person!" she shrieked.

"Look, if she tricks you into having sex with her while I'm gone, you let me know."

Libby pouted, then headed to the locker room. I walked up to the front desk where the three trainers were, still arguing about the primaries.

"It's time we had a female president," Tiffany huffed.

"No way, a black president would do more for the working class," Manny rebutted.

"Hey, guys," I interrupted them. "No politics at the front desk please; Manny, you know most of our clients are conservatives." I turned to Jacob, "When Libby comes out of the locker room she can have a smoothie, but *not* the peanut butter cup one, OK? It's got too much sugar and that's what keeps upsetting her IBS. So, no matter how much she whines or pleads, just protein and water, and you can tell her I said so."

Libby popped her head out of the locker room and shouted to the front desk, "There aren't any towels in here! And somebody clogged the toilet!"

"I can't believe she clogged that thing again," Manny said in amazement. "That's the third time in two weeks!"

"I think she does it on purpose," Jacob confirmed.

"Hey, Tiff," I said as a horrified look swept over her face, "can you please handle that while I go grab some towels from the back?"

"Aw, why me?" The other trainers chuckled.

"Because it's the women's room." I pointed to Manny and Jacob. "Would you want either of these characters lurking around in there while *you* were in the shower?"

Manny handed Tiffany the plunger.

I swung the men's locker room door open to see Tom—who at seventy-eight years old was the gym's oldest member—standing buck naked with one leg propped up on the sink, using a blow-dryer on his genitals. He casually turned to me and shouted over the blow-dryer, "Hey, Jeff, do you think I could book some time with you when you get back from Columbus? I could really use some help."

"Well, that depends," I yelled back. "Is this how you dress for a workout?" He laughed as I smacked him on the back.

I grabbed the overflowing hamper and swapped the dirty towels out with a batch fresh out of the dryer. I took my time folding them, enjoying the few minutes of solitude.

On my way back from the laundry room, I popped my head into the control room and, on the security camera, saw Kane, one of the trainers, trapped under the bench press, struggling to push the bar off of his chest. I dropped the laundry basket and sprinted up the back hall, dashed through the locker room, rushing past naked Tom, and out onto the gym floor. I zipped across the room and helped lift the bar off of Kane. "What the fuck were you thinking, man?!" I asked him, "You know you don't use clips when you're working out alone!"

"I really thought I had it for a minute, there," Kane said as his face started returning to its normal color.

Once I saw he was OK, I lightened up. "Just do me a favor," I said while helping him off the bench, "until you get enough muscle to lift these weights, don't use the clips again."

"Oh, ha-ha," he mocked me.

"And while you're resting," I said, "do me another favor and grab the basket of towels from the back hall and hand them to Tiff—."

"Hey, Jeff!" I heard a woman's voice behind me. "We're here!" I turned to see my friend Natalie from WSLS and her camera guy lugging their equipment through the front door. "Thanks so much for doing this; we had a last-minute cancelation."

"Uh, it's OK, but, just so you know, I've got a client coming in any minute now, so we'll have to work around that."

"No problem," she confirmed. "We'll just ask you a couple of questions while you're training and then we can dub whatever we need to over the shots afterward."

As they began setting up their lights, my last client—my young, very attractive client—Carrie had already warmed up and was waiting for me on the leg press machine. I walked over to join her.

As she pressed her legs straight up into the air and slowly retracted them, bringing her thighs all the way against her chest, I couldn't help noticing that, as usual, she wasn't wearing any under-wear. I did my best not to look down, but it didn't help that she showed up for her workouts exclusively wearing tennis skirts.

She grabbed my hand and placed it on her thigh. "Could you help spot me, in case my muscles give out?"

"Actually," I repositioned my hand on the top of the leg press machine, "I've got much better leverage to secure the weight from up here."

It always took some serious willpower to maintain my professionalism throughout our sessions, but this time it wasn't about me; I had to get her covered up so that her naked bottom half wouldn't be all over daytime television.

"Carrie, let's get through this exercise quickly, please; that news crew over there is going to record us working out in a minute." I sweated far more than she did during her final sets on the leg press, after which I guided her to the other side of the gym while the camera guy miked me up.

"Jeff, can you count to ten for sound check?" the camera guy asked.

"Sure: one, two, three, four, five—"

"OK, we're good!" he stopped me. "Whenever you're ready, Nat."

Then Natalie began talking into the camera. "Today on Fit & Fab, we follow local fitness guru, Jeff Scot Philips, into the gym to learn his secret formula for weight loss." Then she turned to me, "Jeff, tell us, how do your clients keep getting such great results?"

"I'm so sorry, Natalie; can you hang on one second? *Guys!*" I shouted at the front desk, "Will someone please ring up Tom—he's been standing there for, like, five minutes."

"Cut it," the cameraman mumbled.

"OK, let's go from the top." Natalie faced back to the camera. "Today on *Fit & Fab*, we head into the gym to learn Jeff Scot Philips's secret weight-loss formula." Then back to me. "Jeff, what's your trick for helping people lose so much weight?"

"Well, Natalie," I began answering while I watched Libby behind the camera grabbing a giant brown smoothie from Jacob's hand, "the most important thing to remember is that—*Jacob!*" I shouted at the front desk again. "What did I tell you about giving her the peanut butter cup one?"

"Too late. He already made it," Libby smirked.

"This isn't a game, guys!" I shouted at both of them. "Libby's health," I pointed at her, "and *your* goddamn medical bills are on the line, and I seem to be the only one who gives a shit!"

"Are you getting this?" Natalie asked her camera guy.

"Oh, lighten up." Jacob fired back. "It's just *one* smoothie."

"That's a good point," I said sarcastically. "It is just one smoothie, and, in fact, from now on, the next person to give Libby *one* peanut butter cup smoothie is on toilet patrol." Jacob's head sank as Manny ribbed him with a soft elbow to the stomach.

I turned back to Natalie. "All right, good to go."

"OK," she said. "Why don't you just dive into telling us what your secret is."

"Sure. The most important thing I teach my clients up front," I continued as I checked on Carrie, "is that results don't come from just—*whoa, whoa, whoa!*" I spun around.

I caught Carrie just as she was climbing into the adductor—the exercise machine where you sit with your legs spread in a split formation and you open and close them to strengthen the inner thigh muscles—and guided her to a machine positioned farther away from us. Manny and Jacob snapped their fingers in disappointment.

By the end of Carrie's workout, and after another handful-or-so of outtakes, Natalie was able to piece enough footage together for her segment. As they were packing up, Carrie popped her head out of the locker room to shout to me, "Hey, Jeff, there aren't any towels and I'm hopping in the shower; can you bring me one?!"

I turned to Tiffany. "That's all you, Tiff. *Wait*, how the hell are there no towels left?"

"Well," Tiffany nervously smiled, "I had to use most of them to soak up the water around the toilet."

I turned to Manny and Jacob. "Are you guys going to survive while I'm away this weekend?"

"Don't worry about this place," Manny assured me. "We've got it under control."

Not fully believing him, but also not having much of a choice, I handed Manny my office key and headed home to pack my bags for Ohio.

When I arrived in Columbus for the annual fitness expo, which brought in 155,000 fans and 17,000 athletes from around the world, the downtown streets were packed with people. I was giddy, as one of my boyhood dreams was about to come true. I was on my way to meet the Austrian Oak, the Governator, the record-breaking seven-time Mr. Olympia, and my idol since childhood: Arnold Schwarzenegger.

The Arnold Classic was a three-day event consisting of a fitness expo with all kinds of sideshows—like a world's strongest man challenge, an archery competition, swimsuit contests, and the bodybuilding competition, whose winner took home $130,000—and then an exclusive VIP banquet, which my expensive ticket granted me access to. The after-party banquet resembled a fancy nightclub: a dark room with a cash bar on either end, excessively loud music, strobe lights, and a fancy buffet winding around the perimeter of the room. After an hour or so, the superstar entered the room surrounded by what looked like a dozen security guards, and I flocked to join the circle of muscular fans surrounding the governor of "Culiforneeah" in hopes of acquiring some of his wisdom. I was decently muscular, just like everyone else standing in the circle, but we all wanted to find out how we too could look like the 1975 Arnold, whose dancing pecks made the Incredible Hulk, Lou Ferrigno, look like a little boy standing beside him onstage. We all stood silently as the god of bodybuilding spoke.

I pushed my way closer to the middle, as Arnie was in the midst of quoting lines from one of his early movies, *Pumping Iron*, in his exaggerated Austrian accent. "To me, exercise feels like cumming—you know, like when you're with a woman. I'm cumming at home; I'm cumming in the gym—every day I'm in heaven!" Or, when someone asked him whether he drank milk for the protein, he responded, "Milk is for babies; if you want to be a man, you've got to drink beer." Because of silly little statements like these, it was impossible to distinguish between Arnold being serious and Arnold being goofy, so the entire circle of fans around him still thought he was joking when he said, "If you want to weigh two hundred and fifty pounds of muscle, you've got to eat two hundred and fifty grams of meat every day."

For some reason, that statement jumped out at me.

Everyone else laughed, but to me it wasn't *quite* ridiculous-sounding enough to serve as an Arnie joke. It seemed like a plausible nugget of truth.

The first thing I did when I got back to Virginia was measure and prepare all my food for the entire week in advance, instead of trying to count every gram of protein I would be eating for each meal. I spent all day Sunday baking chicken, grilling sirloins, pan-frying cod and tuna steaks, hard-boiling eggs, and then using a scale to weigh out each meal. By portioning my steak meals to six ounces, my chicken meals to eight ounces, and my cod and tuna meals to ten ounces I could be sure each one contained fifty grams of protein. All I had to do to get my required two hundred and fifty grams was eat five of these preweighed meals each day.

Sure enough, after one year of changing nothing but my diet—specifically my protein consumption—I shot up from one hundred and ninety pounds to two hundred and fifty pounds of muscle weight. And, to my delight, my new body also came with an unexpected bonus; I finally had a six pack! *How the hell did this happen? I'm eating more than ever!*

I was elated—not only had I discovered how to pile on muscle, but I also seemingly uncovered the secret to fat loss, and I made it my mission to share it with everyone. I got certified as a nutritionist so that I could better understand the science behind my discovery, and how to best relay this new knowledge to my clients and educate them on how to eat like me.

Before, my approach to helping clients lose weight was based on getting them to cut out anything that wasn't real food—pretty much anything that came in a wrapper or box—and to get them solely eating things like meat, vegetables, and grains. This approach worked pretty well for most of them, but it was far from systematic and was riddled with all sorts of inconsistencies. For example, my client Libby weighed two hundred and twenty-five pounds and wanted to get down to one eighty, while my client Robyn was at about one hundred and twenty pounds and only needed to get down to one ten, for a women's figure competition. Telling them both to eat protein and veggies would produce wildly different results for each of them, even if they ate the exact same things. Before the Arnold Classic, I didn't know that by matching the number of protein grams a person eats to their body weight and lean mass that their fat and muscle levels would adjust accordingly; that Robyn would get more predictable results if she specifically ate four ounces of chicken—or an equivalent meat portion—three times a day, while Libby would do better to have five ounces of chicken four times per day.

Unfortunately my clients didn't take to this new diet technique as readily as I had; they simply didn't have the time, couldn't afford it, or, mostly, were just too lethargic to prepare their meals and eat the way I did. So I started seeking solutions for them. I started designing weight-loss programs and selling them as an add-on service through the studio. For two hundred dollars a pop, I would provide clients with a step-by-step food prep booklet—a detailed grocery list, a cooking procedure breakdown with recipes, and a labeling system that assigned each meal to a given day and time. This was a complete waste of time, because not a single person actually followed the instructions laid out for them. Then I tried partnering with an in-home chef who would visit my clients' houses and cook all their meals for them. He couldn't handle the workload; in fact he actually bitched that I was pushing *too* many clients on him.

Next, some of my clients tried ordering Nutrisystem's "food" and matching it to the program I'd designed for them, but when Libby brought me one of her meals to try—a pathetic little turkey sausage suffocating in a plastic film with no nutrition label indicating what was in it (though it was clearly jam-packed with so many chemicals it could sit on the shelf for months at room temperature and still be eaten, but probably not digested)—it became evident to me what the problem was. The *real* reason why my clients were struggling with their weight was because they were being duped into thinking that *this* sort of thing was healthy for them. I didn't blame Pizza Hut or Frito Lays—nobody ate that kind of stuff thinking it's good for them. The real enemies were the Nutrisystems of the world.

I couldn't find a single damn company offering a solution to my clients' problems.

Sitting at my dining room table on a chilly Sunday morning, brainstorming ways to help my clients achieve their weight-loss goals, it hit me that they desperately wanted to eat the way I told them to. They were even willing to pay someone else to prepare their food, so, I thought, "Why don't I do it?"

Bingo!

I would create the anti-Nutrisystem: a food company that pre-pared edible food *and* actually cared about the customers. If Nutri-system was Microsoft, then I was going to be Apple. I even took it a step further. I pinned that turkey sausage that Libby had brought me on my office wall and kept it there as a reminder of the enemy I had to save the people from.

I was already planning to cook my meals for the entire week that day, so why not buy in bulk, prepare all the food at my place, and pocket the difference? I wasn't a fan of cooking and I had zero culinary acumen, but once I got the ball rolling, I could hire people with kitchen skills to do the food prep for me. I called my ten most loyal clients and asked for their grocery money so that I could do

their shopping for them, prepare their meals for the entire week, and deliver their food later that evening.

Fit Food was born.

I spent all Sunday afternoon in my tiny, steamy kitchen with timers going off, smoke seeping from the oven, all four spider burners being abused—the front two held frying pans loaded with my soon-to-be-famous tuna cakes, while the back burners hosted two giant pots full of hard-boiled eggs with the water boiling to the brim—my George Foreman grill overflowing the useless little grease trap underneath it, and a rapidly diminishing twelve pack in the fridge. When all the food was cooked, I measured and organized the portions according to each individual's specifications: one-hundred-forty-five-pound Caroline would get four ounces of chicken along with a three-quarter cup of veggies for Monday's and Thursday's lunches. Michelle, on the other hand, was one-hundred-thirty-pound ER nurse and competitive athlete who was preparing for a figure competition, a less muscular version of a bodybuilding competition, but more toned than a bikini competition; she needed six ounces of chicken with a cup and a half veggies *plus* a cup of slow starch in the form of brown rice for her lunches. The meals were labeled by day and meal: "Monday, breakfast," "Wednesday, afternoon snack." There was no thinking required, just reheat and eat. At the end of the day, I wasn't just handing my clients prepared meals; I was giving them a weight-loss and muscle-toning system, specific to each individual.

At the end of the week, when I called to ask how everyone was enjoying his or her food, every single client told me he or she had lost seven pounds over the last seven days. At first I thought they'd all conspired and were fucking with me. "Seven pounds in just one week? You guys might have had me if you'd said three or four pounds," I granted. "Or *maaaybe* if one or two of you lost a little more . . . but, come on, every single one of you lost *seven* pounds?! Not buying it." But when I met them for their weigh-in and used skinfold calipers to contrast their BMI against their body fat percentage, sure enough, they'd all lost the exact same amount: seven pounds of body fat.

After some research, I found out that I'd unknowingly put them into a biological process called ketosis, which, when done correctly, can cause a person to lose one pound of body fat each day until they reach their body's ideal weight. It also gives a person tons of energy, which I was noticing in my clients, because the body starts burning fat for fuel instead of blood sugar, like it usually does. This, FYI, makes ketosis extremely helpful for type 2 diabetics, because their bodies struggle to process the sugar in their blood.

I quickly collected testimonials from everyone—affirmation statements, pictures of them on the scale, and, most important, pictures of them eating my meals—then started touting the slogan "Lose 7 Lbs. in 7 Days" on flyers that I posted all over downtown, on a full-page ad in the most prominent women's magazine in the city, and on news and talk show segments. My phone started lighting up. Before I knew it I had so many people placing orders, I started to panic, because I knew I wouldn't be able to handle cooking such large quantities of food alone in my tiny kitchen.

It was time to hire some help.

2

INFILTRATING
WEIGHT WATCHERS

"What a shit hole!"

This was the first sentence that Chef Kevin ever spoke to me. I had just opened the door to reveal the new kitchen that I was interviewing him to manage. As he wandered around the room, the second thing I noticed about Chef Kevin—the first having been his charm—was that he was Jep Robertson's, of *Duck Dynasty*, perfect doppelgänger. He had a black Amish-style beard, black-rimmed glasses, and long black hair suppressed under a baseball cap. But what really stood out to me was his little frame. The saying goes "Never trust a skinny chef." Kevin, at five-ten, couldn't have weighed more than a buck thirty, which made me question whether he even ate food. But I was in desperate need of someone who could dazzle up the menu, so I invited him in.

I'd recently found a kitchen that had been built for cooking shows and culinary classes, not for pumping out hundreds of meals each day, but since that business wasn't doing so well I worked a deal with the owner who agreed to quadruple all the appliances. What we ended up with looked like what you'd get if Emeril Lagasse's kitchen mated with a Sears showroom: The thick marble countertops were offset by the eight convection ovens; the carpeted seating area with the bar-style serving table was canceled out by the five loud refrigerators and giant deep freezer; and the air of elegance that the shiny utensils and top-brand knife set gave off was overshadowed by the big industrial roller racks, about a hundred cooking trays, and what seemed like a million little hand towels coalescing into a mountain in the corner.

While Chef Kevin moped around the room, balking at every aspect of it—"These knives are shit. There aren't enough hand towels. What kind of fucking idiot puts carpet in a kitchen?"—I quizzed him on his credentials.

"So where'd you get your culinary degree from?"

"Virginia Tech."

"Oh, no shit; go Hokies!"

"Fuck the Hokies. I hope UVA stomp their asses this year."

"OK . . . so, where was your last job?"

"That fuckin' sports bar on Main Street with the watered-down beer and chips as a side dish." He continued inspecting the equipment. "This thermometer's shit; you'll need to get me a nicer one."

"So, why a sports bar? Seems like with your background you'd be more at home designing the menu at a high-end restaurant."

"Nobody's offered me the position yet—pricks don't recognize talent when they see it. Where'd you get these pans, a garage sale?"

I handed him a list of the meals I'd been cooking. "So, what do you think about the menu? Got any thoughts on how to improve it?"

Without looking at it, he handed it back to me. "Yeah, roll it up and put it on the spinning rack beside the toilet. I'm going to need to redo everything."

Chef Kevin had been referred to me through a good friend who assured me, "I'm tellin' ya, if you can get past his 'tude, the guy's a wizard in the kitchen."

"Ha!" I couldn't help laughing at his brazenness. "Well, yeah, that sounds great."

He finished his walk-through, turned to face me, and shrugged.

I fanned my arms out. "So what do you think?"

"Well, you've got quite the shit hole here."

"Well, if you're up to the task," I said, "it's your shit hole now."

My friend was right; Chef Kevin performed miracles with the menu. He transformed a basic sirloin into "balsamic-glaze London broil on top of steamed broccoli and roasted garlic." The pork chops became "pork loin asado with cilantro-lime mojo nestled beside a sweet potato–butternut hash." The scrambled eggs were now a "vegetable frittata with cinnamon-blueberry porridge on the side." And the tilapia was upgraded to "Cajun tilapia surrounded by a blend of apples and olive-oil-roasted kale."

NutriSystem, eat your fucking heart out!

He was creating meals that even someone like me, a guy with a total indifference to taste or texture, couldn't help falling in love with. After he used basic herbs and spices to transition my lightly seasoned chicken breast into "grilled chicken pomodoro with roasted tomato and haricots verts," and punched me in the taste buds with his creamy, fresh tomato sauce with sprinkled basil, he'd sold me. Clients liked my food before; now, they would become raving fans.

I wasn't just impressed by the amazing-tasting new menu; Chef Kevin also had an intimate understanding of temperatures and would cook each dish to a specific prefreezing temperature so that, when customers reheated it, it was perfectly cooked: the chicken was still juicy, and the steak was still tender and pink on the inside.

He also had an amazing kitchen management system. Before, when I was buying groceries, I would just guess the quantity of each item I needed, and if I ran short of something, I'd run back to the grocery store. But Kevin somehow intuitively knew the math for exactly how many eggs, for example, he would need to make five hundred vegetable frittatas, and he knew which purveyors would deliver on which days and kept a timely inventory sheet so our stock would never run out. But he wouldn't sit for too long, either.

The character trait that really won me over was Kevin's in-depth understanding of cost—how he designed each menu item with profit margins in mind. All these incredible dishes that he'd been concocting were no more expensive than my original plain, shitty ones. I'd found my guy.

After a couple of weeks of Kevin running the show, word was getting out about our astonishing new menu, and more and more orders were coming in—fifty, seventy-five, a hundred orders for a week's worth of food apiece—which caused two huge problems. To begin with, the two of us alone simply couldn't handle the workload and we were getting behind on deliveries. Even worse, customers were complaining that they were missing meals in almost every order and/or I'd given them some incorrect meals. This made sense to me statistically, because if you think about how many orders a restaurant gets wrong on a given night and then multiply that by thirty-five, seventy, or one hundred and forty meals—depending on whether our customers wanted one week's, two weeks', or a month's worth of food—there could be a lot of potential errors per each customer order. The only way to fix these problems was to have more eyeballs on each order and more hands in the kitchen, so I worked with Chef Kevin to recruit a sous chef and some line cooks to work under him.

First, I found Barbara, a.k.a. Chef Babs, a.k.a. Hurricane Babs, whose neurotic tendencies (her inability to let a timer or buzzer go unanswered for more than two seconds) and obsessive compulsive behaviors (the urge to keep all utensils clean, to the point of sometimes taking one out of your hand, miduse, so she could wash and return it) made her accident-prone on steroids. She also had a weird thing about cotton balls and swabs, to the point that, to her, just the thought of someone squeezing a handful of them was like nails on a chalkboard. Then, there was Chef Casey, whom I'd found on Craigslist—a mistake I'll never make again. A good ol' country-fried dude, he loved to recite all the latest fantasy football stats, tell racist, sexist, and pull-my-finger jokes. Donavon and Seth were the only ones younger than I was, both in their teens and both showed up to work every day stoned off their asses. Neither of them had any real culinary experience, but because they didn't have that typical *I'm a chef—now bow to me* chip on their shoulder, they turned out to be the hardest workers of all. And last, but certainly not least, was my longtime friend Dave. He and I had become personal trainers at the same time, and he'd helped me open Fit Studio: from construction to designing the layout to picking out the exercise equipment to the grand opening. Dave was the jack-of-all-trades kind of guy you could call in a pinch and he'd be there, no matter what.

Monday morning, I showed up to the kitchen to meet the U.S. Foods delivery driver, with my car packed to the roof with boxes of food from Sam's Club. All the chefs and cooks—except for Casey, who was nowhere to be seen—met us in the parking lot to form an impromptu assembly line as we began unloading the boxes of tomatoes, satchels of onions, chicken breasts, ground beef, egg cartons, drums of olive oil, and packages with a couple of thousand resealable containers, and started hauling them up the stairs. When everything was inside, I printed off the order sheets and everything went into motion, each person manning two or three stations at once.

Babs was at the stove beside Kevin, sautéing the jambalaya ingredients in a pan, and as it sat, she would turn to dice up some vegetables—her eyes started watering terribly as she sliced her way through the giant onions—while she attempted to cheerily quiz Kevin on his culinary background. She had bypassed a culinary degree and had gotten a job cooking at Outback Steakhouse, so she was curious to learn what bonus skills Kevin had acquired in school. Kevin was adding spices to the sauces that went on top of the various chicken dishes—curry sauce for the ginger Indian chicken, pesto sauce for the Italian herb and Parmesan chicken, and a mild hot sauce for the buffalo chicken—as he simultaneously glazed the pork tenderloin before it was slow roasted in the oven and repeatedly told Babs to fuck off.

I was leaning over the giant aluminum table in the center of the room, forming the ground beef into burger patties for Dave to cook on the grill, after which I dumped a dozen pounds of ground turkey into a giant mixing bowl and stuck my hands into the freezing cold meat to mix all the ingredients together. Then I used an ice cream scoop to form turkey meatballs and set them in the oven to bake. Dave, the grill master, put the salmon into the oven to precook it before grilling it—a little trick Kevin showed us to make each fillet consistent—then fired up the grill, where he'd put lines on the burgers I'd formed for him. As soon as the burgers were done, he'd spray the grill down with Pam and throw the salmon on for a minute or two to add some grill marks and smoky flavor to each of the bright pink fillets.

Seth dipped broccoli and cauliflower into giant pots of boiling water to blanch them, dumped dozens of eggs into two other pots to be hard-boiled, then he pulled out a knife and started cutting the fat off of the chicken, and set it in the oven to precook it before Dave would slap it on the grill to finish it off. Donavon sprinkled Kevin's Cajun blend on top of the tilapia and set it in the oven, then opened up all the giant Bumble Bee cans of tuna, drained the water, mixed the fish with egg yolks, spices, and oatmeal—as a healthier binding alternative to bread crumbs—and then weighed out four, five, and six ounce tuna cakes that Babs would fry on the stovetop when her jambalaya was done.

Casey was supposed to be mixing the protein brownies and the carb-free pizza dough, but given that he was MIA, Donavon took over the pizza project and I went to work on the brownies.

Around midday, I lifted my head up from the whey protein and peanut butter mixture to see how everyone was doing: Babs was pinching her cell phone between her ear and shoulder to fight with the bank over her credit score, intermittently leaning her head back to sniffle as she diced the onions with her jittery little fingers.

Dave was running through the door every couple of minutes with two giant trays of chicken he'd just pulled off the grill, setting them in front of Kevin and asking whether he'd help him carry the next two big trays in, to which Kevin repeatedly told him, "Fuck outta here!" Dave would then swing by Donavon at the stove, and they'd trade jokes about anomalous bodily functions and laugh their asses off. Kevin and Seth—whom Kevin had poached from the sports bar he worked at—were in the corner having an intense debate about who would give a more sensual BJ: "that topless Miley Cyrus girl or that new Justin Bieber kid wearing a wig?" Kevin diced the chicken that Dave had brought him and applied his sauces, then Seth placed handfuls of the chicken into containers, and weighed them to match each client's specifications.

I shaped the protein brownies by hand. Still on the phone with the bank, Bab raised her voice, "But that's not fair. My score drops every time you check it, so, please, stop check—!" Her sentence was cut short by a loud scream.

Blood was gushing from Babs's finger onto the cutting table. A thick slab of skin dangled from where she had sliced the inside of her thumb. Everyone rushed to help her stop the bleeding—except Kevin, who sat mumbling, "What a fucking idiot" just loud enough for everyone to hear. After some rinsing, peroxiding—though without cotton swabs, of course—and a hell of a lot of gauze, we were able to stop the bleeding and calm Babs down.

Right about the time we'd gotten Babs's thumb mummified, the kitchen door swung open and Chef Casey came lethargically strolling through, whistling "Sweet Child of Mine."

"Mornin', folks," he addressed us with a little salute as he tied his apron on. It was approaching lunchtime, and when Casey made eye contact with me, I waved for him to follow me into the office, so as not to make a scene.

"Casey, you know we started at nine a.m., right?" I asked.

"Oh . . . well . . . I'm sorry, man," he said. "I just had some emergency stuff I had to take care of."

"Everyone's getting ready to punch out for lunch; they already did your morning work for you."

"Well, I already ate before I came in, so I can get a jump on this afternoon's work, if you want."

"Casey, I need to know this isn't going to happen again, buddy. This whole operation only works if everyone shows up on time and works together. I'm counting on you—we're all counting on you—so please don't let us down again."

"I know. I said I was sorry."

"Don't say it to me; tell it to them."

We walked back into the kitchen, and everybody had already headed out to lunch except Chef Kevin, who was standing in the doorway with a prelunch cigarette, so Casey extended his hand to him and said, "Nice to meet you, chef; I'm Casey. Sorry I was running behind today—family emergency."

Kevin left Casey's hand dangling awkwardly in space as he exhaled a cloud of smoke into his face and said, "Fuck outta my way," and then walked down the steps.

Casey turned back to look at me, and I just smiled and said, "What do you think of your new boss?"

After lunch, Dave went back to running trays up and down the stairs as he manned the grill, and Kevin and Seth continued to dice, sauce, and portion whatever Dave handed them as they strategized all the illegal substances they were going to smuggle into Bonnaroo this year. Casey was making amends with Donavon by sharing one of his "a priest and a rabbi walk into a bar" jokes. Babs, who'd returned from lunch with a wicked case of Jimmy legs and arms, picked up a pot full of boiling water with her bare hands, screamed at the top of her lungs, and then dropped it onto the floor, ruining two dozen eggs.

Most of the afternoon, I was on my Bluetooth, taking orders while timing different methods of making the turkey meatballs; they were by far the slowest process in the kitchen and they were holding up everything. By scooping each individual meatball, it took about twenty minutes per eighty balls, but I discovered that, if I spread the mixture flat across a cooking tray, then used a pizza slicer to cut them into rows *before* baking, they would naturally balloon up in the oven, and when they came out, I'd have a tray full of little balls that had only taken about sixty seconds to form.

As I tested and documented the process, I concluded that because there are sixteen ounces in a pound, and you can fit five pounds of meat per tray, if I sliced the mixture into rows of eight-by-ten, then each ball weighed exactly one ounce, which eliminated the need to weigh each individual meal. We would just put four meatballs for a four ounce portion, six balls for a six ounce portion, etc. This little revelation streamlined the turkey meatball process from two hours and fifteen minutes per one hundred and twenty-five orders down to seventeen minutes!

I started testing ways to speed up all our other processes. I discovered that I was able to chop off a hundred burger patties in twenty-six minutes by spreading the ground beef across a cutting board, cutting it into rows, and then using a cookie-cutter mold to round the edges; I did the same with the tuna cakes. I also figured out that if we used three people in an assembly line per one multistep project, we chopped our time in half, *again*. For example, instead of Donavon making the tuna cakes while I made the turkey meatballs and Casey made the pizza dough, we would all three collaborate on the tuna cakes. Casey opened and drained the tuna cans and handed them off to Donavon, who mixed the ingredients together while Casey began opening up the packages of ground turkey. Then Donavon handed the tuna mixture to me and I spread it across the cutting board and sliced it into rows and handed them off to the stove master, Babs, while Donavon took the ground turkey from Casey and mixed the ingredients in a bowl, and Casey started on the pizza dough. When Donavon handed me the turkey mixture, I spread it onto a tray, cut it, and tossed it into the oven as Donavon blended the pizza dough, and so on, and so on.

Toward the end of the day, when all the food was finished, Kevin and Babs began cleaning the kitchen while I handed out checklists to the rest of the crew, and then we began filling the orders. I turned to Dave and read the first order, "Mrs. Smith: seven four-ounce tuna cakes, four five-ounce turkey meatballs, twelve four-ounce balsamic steaks, twelve six-ounce protein brownies." Dave would zip through the rows of tables, count out the meals, and mark them off his sheet, then hand them to Casey who would count them a third time as he placed them in the client's thermal delivery bag.

Initially, everyone thought this triple-check process was overly redundant. "Why do we need three sheets per order? Why can't one person read the list and pull the orders, and the bagger check behind him?" Casey whined. Back when it was just Kevin and me, even two pairs of eyes didn't catch all the mistakes. By adding that third pair of eyes to the packing process, the errors miraculously disappeared.

After all the orders were filled, we compared our sheets for a final check, to make sure there were no discrepancies, then handed them off to the runners—a couple of youngsters who showed up at the end of each day for a hundred bucks plus whatever tips they might get—who delivered them to the customers' houses.

About six months into this little food venture, we ran into a bottleneck. The excruciating detail that each new customer required became very time-consuming, because I had to interview and assess each person, work my algorithms on his or her specific macronutrient requirements, and then design a personalized nutrition blueprint. Once I'd reached the limit of how many meal plans I could design each week, I would start pushing any incoming orders over to the next week, which annoyed the eager customers.

Everyone was seeing great results because of our diet formula—which I didn't want to compromise—but I needed to find a way to expedite the process, so that each customer would still get a unique experience without me having to create a detailed program for each one. Then I got an idea.

My old client, Libby, routinely and unsolicitedly called to inform me of how unacceptably the gym was doing under Manny's command. This particular week, I decided to redirect her spying to a more useful cause.

"Jeff," she whined, "the new girl, Erin, that Manny hired to replace Tiffany . . . she's too butch."

"Libby . . ."

"She looks like a tomboy—cargo pants and baggy T-shirts."

"Libby!"

"She's like a drill sergeant. I think the other gym members will be gross—"

"*Libby*!" I interrupted her. "You can tell me more about that later, but right now, I need to ask you for a favor. I need someone sneaky, someone I can trust, whom I can send into the Weight Watchers program to pretend to be a customer, but all the while secretly gather information to report back to me."

By her whispery tone, I could tell she'd already accepted the mission. "What kind of information would you need me to find out?"

"Everything!"

"Everything?"

"Yes. I need to know all their sales tactics."

"Uh-huh."

"The hooks that keep customers buying their products."

"Yeah. Yeah."

"And, possibly most importantly, I need you to find out how they give each person a unique experience."

"Oh, I can definitely do that!"

Libby was the perfect person for the task because she was so *frustratingly* resilient, so *painfully* stubborn, that, regardless of how much weight she needed to lose, I knew she would never accept a health professional's advice without an epic battle. The more resistant she acted, the more I would learn from hearing how the Weight Watchers staff handled her.

"So what exactly do you want me to do?"

"Your objective is simple." I said as if briefing a soldier to go into battle. "Be yourself."

After a couple of months of infiltrating enemy territory, Libby met me at the gym to defect, toting a giant box full of printed material, notes, and, most important, her audio recordings from the weekly meetings. The only annoying part was that, throughout each meeting, she would mash the recorder up against her lips and, like a spy who confused gossip for intelligence, burble things like "It's confirmed: Janet bats for the other team." Over hours of recordings, spanning months of group meetings, she updated me on the alleged sexual orientation of her point-counting peers.

I'd be listening to the audio, trying to take notes, and, out of nowhere, I'd hear Libby whisper, "Oh, Dawn and Lexi are definitely lovers."

But in between her homophobic espionage reports, her back and forths with the meeting leaders were producing some excellent insights. As I listened to the tapes, each week, she gave comical issues and excuses that the Weight Watchers crew had to overcome. The more ridiculous Libby got, the more sales tactics I learned, as I listened to the frustrated WW staff work their way through their product-pushing scripts.

After one week on the WW food, Libby gave them some lovely feedback. "Your meals gave me bad diarrhea."

The poor WW staffer smoothly maneuvered Libby's intestinal issue into a product pitch. "Well, nobody knows your body better than you; maybe you should purchase our kit for preparing your own food, along with our cookbook."

Then Libby came back the following week with "All the meals I prepared were too much to keep track of; I got flustered and ended up eating a bunch of Reese's."

The WW solution: "I recommend our storage package; it makes it super simple to organize your meals."

Libby returned, "OK, I cooked all my own meals—within the points system—and fed some of it to my cat who got sick. You owe me a partial refund, because the vet bill was expensive and I still didn't lose weight."

"Tell you what," said the meeting leader, trying not to let her laughter escape, "I know how horrified I would be if my cat were sick, so I'm going to credit half of your purchase back. And sometimes diet alone can't do the trick. Sounds like you need to get your metabolism revved up too. Why don't you try our exercise DVD, along with some of our workout equipment? This way, you don't even have to leave the comfort of your home."

Then a vintage Libby claim: "OK, I was following the DVD, and it hurt my knee."

Amazingly, they turned this into an opportunity to sell her something else. "I'm so sorry about your knee. I can tell you're clearly a hard worker, so it sounds to me like you just need a little extra accountability, someone to support you on a more personal level. Let's set you up with a coach for the next couple of weeks; she'll help you reach your goal."

I didn't know how Libby was going to get past a personal coach, but after one week, sure enough, she delivered.

"I get the feeling that my coach is a lesbian. I'm not comfortable working with her."

The stunned WW staffer was too terrified to respond directly to her concern, so she just went right into her pitch: "Why don't you just try using the points system, on your own, with whatever foods you choose for the next week, and we'll see how you do."

One week later, Libby said, "Well, I did lose weight last week, but I feel funny, sometimes dizzy, and my sex drive has gone down." I couldn't help shuddering at the thought.

The Weight Watchers rebuttal was "Why don't you check with your doctor? If everything is OK, we'll ease you back on to some of the Weight Watchers meals—ones that don't irritate your stomach— and monitor your results very closely."

Libby returned. "My bad diarrhea came back again."

In addition to the excellent entertainment—what a fucking treasure trove these tapes were!—Weight Watchers did a damn good job of keeping her in the selling loop with all sorts of sneaky techniques.

First, these little meetings were ingenious.

It quickly became evident to me that WW wasn't actually about the points system—or any of the other bullshit its staff was pushing—its foundation was the concept of support. "When Jean Nidetch founded Weight Watchers in 1963," one of the class leaders told the group, "it was nothing more than a tiny social group meeting in her living room each week for support." The brilliance of providing a social safety net was that it was addictive, and Weight Watchers was shrewdly exploiting this.

So, I noted, its first objective was to make customers dependent. This explained why the first meeting was free, because once people were hooked on the support, they would buy into *whatever* their coach threw at them. I took this idea and started a weekly support call for paying customers, which, as a nice bonus, produced instant and consistent revenue.

Then there was the individual coaching. What a clever guise for its salespeople to follow up with customers and engage new prospects. These customers were paying a salesperson to pitch them on the company's products.

And, finally, I learned what an amazing gimmick its points system was.

For Weight Watchers, getting consumers to focus on something other than the actual food they're eating was a very cunning way to get people to buy its products. I listened to them teach Libby that there was no difference between Reese's Pieces and broccoli, according to the points system, and, therefore, she was welcome to continue eating her Reese's—in addition to buying some Weight Watchers snacks—because, as the group leader explained, "they have the same number of points as meat and veggies, but with *much* better taste!" It became evident to me that once a customer had adopted this points gimmick, hook, line, and wallet, Weight Watchers could effortlessly upsell them products in a never-ending loop.

Another juicy gem I learned from listening to the group leaders bragging about their company's size and origin was that Weight Watchers was nothing more than a food company masquerading as a weight-loss company. The company was owned by Heinz, for Christ's sake—the company who owns T.G.I Friday's and makes pizza bagel bites and Oscar Mayer hot dogs!

After learning so much from studying Weight Watchers, I decided to study more diet fads, the companies that started them, and how they were used to increase sales.

The first American diet appeared in 1895; it was called "Fletcherism," named after its creator, Horace Fletcher, who—with zero credentials in science or nutrition—advised people to chew each bite of food one hundred times until it was liquefied in their mouths. This was somehow supposed to help people lose weight. I guess if you want to vomit every time you eat, then you'll consume less and won't gain as much. Other than taking the pleasure out of eating, the Fletcherizing fad didn't have much of an effect on the country, but it *did* inspire the next nutrition mastermind—a name that's no doubt sitting in your cupboard right now—to build an entire industry out of a diet fad.

Inspired by Horace Fletcher's ability to alter the eating habits of the entire country, John Harvey Kellogg decided to create a diet fad of his own. The health reform institute that Kellogg worked at instructed its high-paying patients to eat nothing but fourteen pounds of grapes each day. Just in case the clients didn't find this repulsive enough, for dessert, they received a dairy enema—meaning that the staff shoved yogurt up the patients' asses as a source of protein.

This unaccredited entrepreneur told people this was the healthiest way to eat, and much like today, few people questioned it.

Americans were paying top dollar for this service, and these people weren't mindless lemmings, either; two of his most touted patients were billionaire oil tycoon John D. Rockefeller and the twenty-sixth president of the United States, Teddy Roosevelt—even they were susceptible to marketing power.

In 1906, Kellogg created his first food product, Kellogg's Corn Flakes—the first ready-to-eat cereal in history. He then mounted a vicious marketing campaign against the egg industry, training consumers to stop buying eggs, which he claimed led to heart attacks—a claim backed by zero science—and start buying the better solution, which was his corn-based cereal. Because of this polarizing marketing campaign, his crisps of sugary corn started quickly appearing in houses, stores, and even hospitals across the nation, and fed US troops fighting in WWII.

If a random business owner could legally spout that "eating eggs leads to a heart attack" without any evidence to back it up, what would stop any other food company from doing it? What would stop *me* from doing it?

Lucky for Americans, the protein enema fad didn't survive—talk about an uncomfortable Thanksgiving dinner—but the cereal industry is now a multibillion dollar industry, and most consumers don't buy it because it's smart or convenient, or even because it tastes good. Pay close attention to the message the next time a cereal commercial comes on. Adults buy cereal today because they subconsciously think—thanks to shrewd edutising (advertising disguised as education)—that it has some sort of health benefit. *Source of fiber, source of vitamins and minerals, source of wholesome grains.*

After cornflakes began flooding the marketplace, a new trend sprung into popularity when Lulu Hunt Peters released her book *Diet and Health* in 1918. It was the first weight-loss book to become a best seller by promoting the concept of counting calories. Now, the calorie fad has woven itself into American culture more than any other. This fad was nonsense, but people believed that calories were real and when they wanted to buy low-calorie meals, I could either sell them some or sell nothing at all. In addition to the meals, I also began selling calorie-counting software, wristbands that counted calories, cookbooks with low-calorie recipes, and entire programs dedicated to helping people live a low-calorie lifestyle.

Nobody questioned me. I was able to profit from this one woman's personal philosophy from almost a century ago. The more places people saw a reference to calories, the more it conditioned consumers to believe *"This must be true!"* Even the government bought into it and mandated that calories need to be listed on all food labels. Two scientists were chosen—Merrill and Watt in 1955—to assign calories with numbers, as can be seen in their published study titled "Energy Value of Foods," so that consumers could keep an eye on their consumption, but after years of research leading to inconclusive and random results, the scientists simply had to choose the numbers that we're familiar with today: nine calories per one gram of fat, four calories per one gram of carb or protein. The calorie numbers that were used for food labels, to my enlightenment, were completely made-up! I couldn't believe that all of this information, funded and put together by the Agricultural Research Service—the USDA's in-house research agency—was fully available to the public, and yet nobody seemed to be aware of it.

In 2005, after Oprah helped promote the acai berry as a healthy superfood on her show, she helped Jeremy and Ryan Black spread the acai diet fad across the country, convincing consumers to spend $108 million in just one year. There was a "nicotine diet," propagated by the tobacco companies, which advertised that smoking suppressed appetite. Then the "tapeworm diet" convinced consumers to take pills that allegedly contained live tapeworm parasites, so that people could eat whatever foods they wanted with impunity, because the tapeworms would steal all of their excess calories. Frances Moore Lappé's book, *Diet for a Small Planet,* suggested becoming a vegetarian as a solution for health and weight loss. Do you have any idea how easy and profitable it is to take plain broccoli and carrots, package them as a vegetarian snack, and sell them at a higher price than normal? Speaking of veggies, by pigeonholing a philosophy like veganism into a commodity like juicing, David Wolfe can now sell his NutriBullet blenders for one hundred twenty-nine dollars, even though they are no different from a blender you can get on Amazon .com for fifteen dollars with free shipping.

These fads proved that people would buy *anything*, at *any* price, if you claimed it would slim them down.

As I continued to discover new diet fads, I kept introducing new lines of meals to match them; I made paleo meals for CrossFitters, a carb-cycling nutrition system for bodybuilders, an Eat Right for Your Blood Type program for the people who bought into that sort of thing, an organic, all-natural, low-soy, mercury-free food for our more holistic-minded customers, and, à la Weight Watchers' point-counting gimmick, I devised a color-coded weight-loss plan that my customers could use to choose which of our foods they wanted to eat and still lose weight.

Meals like chicken and steak were blue, which meant they had no carbs; things like our turkey meatballs were yellow, meaning they had a few carbs; and things like our tuna cakes and protein brownies were red, because they were the highest in carbs. The green side dishes were veggies, and purple stood for starches like brown rice and quinoa. So instead of me designing a unique meal plan for every single person, if somebody didn't want to eat chicken and steak every day, for example, he or she could choose to eat our pulled-pork barbecue (blue) for lunch, our chocolate protein brownie (red) as a snack, and our salmon beurre blanc (blue) for dinner; this guaranteed that he or she would consume fewer than twenty grams of carbs without having to keep count, and, most important, without having to consult me about it.

This was the solution I'd been looking for, the formula that would make my business scalable.

The chefs weren't exactly enthused about this color system. "Only a fucktard would ruin food with a dumbass scheme like this" was, I believe, the verbatim response I got from Cryin' Kevin. He felt that assigning colors to meals would too-heavily overshadow his culinary panache, that, instead of appreciating his tasty masterpieces, the customers would now view their meals as a game of Twister. "Third meal: blue; second side dish: purple." But after I let him share his constructive criticism, I reminded him, "I'm the fucktard paying you to cook, so you keep cooking. I'll handle the rest."

Casey whined because applying the Daydots to each meal meant one more thing he had to do. It was challenging enough to get him through the door each morning, so I decided to create a color-coding plan to help him do his job too. "For each meal that gets into a customer's hands without the correct colored sticker on it," I assured him, "your paycheck gets $10 deducted from it."

"That's not fair," he sulked. "What if a sticker falls off during delivery, or if a customer takes the sticker off and claims the meal came without one?"

"Good point . . . you better put *two* stickers on each meal to make sure none of that happens."

My customers, on the other hand, loved the new color-coding system so much that they even used it outside of the program. I would get calls from customers asking, "Hey, I'm at a banquet dinner and I'm down to only one yellow meal left for the day—what color is chicken cordon bleu? Please tell me I can order it!"

People began spreading the word about "this unbelievable new diet, with amazing food, that trims seven pounds of body fat per week!" to their friends and family members, and hundreds of new calls started coming in from other cities and states. Though I knew nothing about the legalities or logistics of shipping food, I was hardly going to turn down their money. After the out-of-state meals were cooked, we froze them and placed them under a block of dry ice inside a Styrofoam cooler, on top of which I'd slap a shipping label and set it out for the FedEx driver to swing by and pick up.

Each day, I would hand the FedEx guy a special meal that I had the chefs prepare just for him, with plastic utensils, a drink, and a napkin. This paid off big time as we continued getting busier—some nights we would be stuffing containers into coolers right up until

FedEx's central hub cutoff time, and I'd call our guy on his cell and ask for a last-minute favor. Never once did he hesitate to zip over and pick up the packages. I repeatedly tried to slip him a twenty for helping us out, but he wouldn't accept the cash; the food was all he wanted.

We were also starting to get a ton of press for our carb-free pizza, lasagna, and chicken poppers—which looked and tasted exactly like Chick-fil-A's nuggets. We had discovered a way to make carb-free pasta and carb-free fried chicken batter just by playing around with different ingredients—the same way we discovered how to make our carb-free pizza dough—and everyone couldn't stop talking about these new meals. We even had a self-proclaimed pizza addict call us and order thirty-five pizza meals for one week; he repeated this for six months and lost one hundred pounds in the process. That story got a lot of attention, and I had to make everyone in the kitchen sign a nondisclosure agreement when I started speaking with the executive chef from Papa John's about potentially selling them our carb-free dough recipe—which I never could bring myself to do.

Just when I thought we couldn't get any busier, a new phenomenon swept the country. Customers started asking, "I'm excited to try your program, but is the food gluten-free?"

I'd read Elisabeth Hasselbeck's book the previous year, and I'd been expecting the hypochondriac tsunami to hit any month. So, even though I knew this was just a senseless fad, I started telling these prospective customers, "You're in luck—we've just added a brand-new gluten-free line!" which, of course, didn't yet exist. After the standard blowback barrage of curses and insults from Cryin' Kevin, he designed the new line of meals, and we were then in the gluten-free business.

After the gluten craze, came CrossFit, whose cult members' obsession with the paleo diet, once again, gave us a giant booster shot. "Sure, our food is paleo." . . . "That's correct; it's gluten-free, too!" . . . "What's that?" . . . "No, we're not like Nutrisystem; we're a million times better—do you want to place an order or not?" The best thing about making paleo meals was that we didn't have to add or subtract anything from our recipes; we just slapped on a paleo label.

As these diet fads grew, we grew right along with them. People all over the East Coast were now calling and orders were coming in faster than I could hire people to cook them. I even started poaching trainer friends from gyms in the area to help out.

The kitchen was a chaotic, stressful food frenzy, and I'm pretty sure we were inadvertently breaking every single health code in existence, because dozens of unqualified food handlers were dancing around, bumping into each other all day, and using abused equipment that looked like it had just returned from war in a kitchen that would barely pass a building inspection, let alone a health one. But thanks to my deal with the Extortion Cougar—I'd begun to look forward to our monthly trysts in my office—I never had to worry about a second kitchen inspection, and because I was handing fistfuls of cash to everyone around me, not a soul was going to complain about anything—except for Cryin' Kevin, of course.

There was more than enough money to make sure everybody stayed happy. After everyone and everything was paid—the chefs, the cooks, the runners, the landlord, the night porter, the food purveyors, inspection "dues," and whatever other fees the owner of the kitchen space constantly shook me down for—I was pocketing eight, nine, ten grand on any given week, and handing hefty bonuses to the crew. We went out and bought new cars, new watches, computers and iPads, and I bought my first property. I even invited a Verizon agent into the kitchen one day and let everybody pick whichever of the latest, fanciest smartphones each of them wanted. But the most exciting thing about our newfound success were the customers' testimonials that just kept piling in.

A guy from Connecticut called to tell us he'd lost thirty pounds; a woman from South Carolina had lost fifty pounds; a guy in southern Virginia had lost just shy of one hundred pounds! One woman gained ten pounds, which was a good thing, her daughter explained, because she couldn't get her eighty-year-old mother to eat her nursing home food and had been worried about her mother's declining weight. A woman in Missouri called to tell us that she used our meals to place second in a figure competition; a woman in Louisiana used them to win a bikini competition; and Miss Virginia was using our food to get in shape for the Miss America pageant. And then, my personal favorite weight-loss success, was my mother, who lost fifty pounds by eating my food; I'd never seen her so energetic and happy in my life!

Some of the most impressive success stories, however, were the handful of customers who'd been calling to report that they were improving their health; some had even reversed diseases that they'd had for years. We seemed to be quite successful at helping people reverse their type 2 diabetes; we frequently received doctor's notes thanking us for helping patients lower their blood pressure and cholesterol. And then there was the one woman who had gone for years unable to walk up stairs without assistance because of an autoimmune disease that was eating away at her knee joints. The high-protein, low-sugar diet had apparently sent her disease into remission, and when she surprised me at the kitchen by walking up the flight of stairs and coming inside to hug me, I had to fight to keep myself from crying along with her.

Fit Food was not only a business success; we were really changing people's lives.

3

HEALTH INDUSTRY RULE NO. 1: THERE ARE NO RULES

"I don't think I can do this."

"You'll be fine," I assured Babs. "Do everything just like we rehearsed it, and you'll do great."

"I'm too nervous," she said. "Please just do it for me."

"Look, I know going on TV for the first time can be terrifying, but that uncomfortable queasiness you feel in your stomach right now, that's completely normal. Pushing through it is what separates the pros from everyone else. And I'm going to be standing right beside you the whole time."

"I've changed my mind. Let Kevin do it."

"He's a kitchen chef, not a TV chef, like you want to be—he doesn't want that kind of attention. The fact of the matter is, the audience wants to hear from *you*!"

"My hands won't stop shaking," she nervously whined. "What if I'm just not cut out for this?"

"You *are* cut out for this. You're a star—you're *my* star—and this is that moment when the world is going to be blown away by the amazing Chef Babs."

"O—OK. *OK!* Yes, I can do this."

"Damn right you can!" I gave her a high five. "Now put that Rachel Ray chick to shame."

The producer counted down from five, the music came on, and the crowd handlers signaled the audience to stand up and start clapping.

"Welcome to *The Hour of Joy!* I'm your host, Joy Sutton, and this morning we're going to be talking about fashion and romance, but first, we're going to learn how to make a healthy lunch that doesn't *taste* healthy—*mmm-hmm!* Now that's my favorite kind of health food! Joining us today in the kitchen is our fitness friend Jeff Scot Philips, along with Chef Babs, from Fit Food."

"So," Joy turned to Babs and me, "what are we making for lunch today?"

"Well, Joy," I said, "We all know how much you love good ol' Southern food. So, today Chef Babs has designed a special menu just for you." I gestured to Babs and it took her an awkward second to realize it was her turn to talk.

"Uh . . . that's right. I'm going to be making crispy fried chicken and cheesy french fries."

"Ooooo," Joy said as she transitioned to a Southern accent. "Dat's what I'm talkin' 'bout!"

Again, Babs hesitated for a half second, so I gently nudged her and she continued, "Oh . . . but, best of all, Joy, they're both zero carbs."

"*Whaaat?* Get out of town, girlfriend!"

"That's right." Babs smiled, getting more comfortable. "Here's how we do it." She began mixing and blending ingredients as she explained each step of the process: ". . . and you coat the chicken in your batter; then I like to sprinkle an extra layer of garlic powder to soak up the moisture before dipping it into the fryer for three minutes."

Then she began making the french fries. "The secret is, instead of potatoes, we use eggplants. The best way to do it is to cut into the center of the eggplant like this," she said as she inserted the knife, "and then spin it around—*Ohhh!*"

Oh, my god. Please tell me she didn't. Hurricane Babs had just sliced open her finger on television, in front of a live studio audience.

"Now folks," I quickly intervened, hastily wrapping a hand towel tightly around her bleeding finger, "this is a little trick Chef Babs likes to use to make me do all the work while she bosses me around," which got everyone, including Babs, to laugh, and took some pressure off of her. "Alright, *boss*," I playfully asked Babs as I finished cutting the eggplant into fry slices, "what should *I* do next?"

With one hand bulkily towel-wrapped, she used her other one to guide me through the recipe. "You'll want to take the pieces of eggplant, dip them in the egg batter, and then roll them through the bowl of shredded cheese." It seemed the audience had already forgotten about the mishap, as Babs continued. "Then, if you want a little extra flavor, you can add a thin layer of the fried chicken batter." I followed along with her instructions. "And then I like to sprinkle just a tiny bit of rosemary and thyme on top before placing them in the oven for twenty minutes at three-fifty."

As we displayed finished versions of the two recipes, a couple of studio interns issued out the premade samples we had brought for the audience so they could taste along with us. Then, just like that, our segment was over; we packed up our equipment, and I drove us back to the kitchen while Babs tended to her finger and repeatedly asked me about her performance—"Are you *sure* I came off confident? I felt like I talked a little too fast. Did I talk too fast?"—I felt proud of her, and truth be told, I felt proud of myself.

We walked through the kitchen door and saw Donavon standing at the deep fryer and Dave sneaking up behind him. He leaned over Don's shoulder and tossed an ice cube into the fryer. It erupted like a firecracker, crackling and spewing drops of three hundred fifty degree oil into the air. Donavon dove backward to take cover, then chased Dave down and punched him in the shoulder. The whole kitchen broke into laughter, except for Casey, who was working quietly as he blended the pizza dough. His face was dark red, which meant he must have just gotten chewed out by Emily.

I had recently hired my longtime friend Emily as my kitchen manager, so I could step out of the kitchen to do things like speeches, sales meetings, and television appearances. A few months before, when I'd left the chefs unattended to give a keynote address at the Civic Center, I returned to the kitchen to discover that Casey had spent the entire day cooking his homemade five-alarm chili and hadn't made a single customer order. Of course, by the time I returned, it was too late to make up the difference, and all the orders were late, which cost us some of our customers.

Emily kept everyone in check, broke up fights between Kevin and whomever he was targeting, documented any Hurricane Babs injuries for potential liability purposes, handled customer service issues, helped me coordinate each month's new menu, and hired and trained the new cooks whom we had to keep bringing on to replace anyone who couldn't handle Kevin's abuse.

"How's the new guy coming along?" I asked Emily.

"Adam's doing fine. He doesn't seem to mind Kevin at all—even when he told him, 'If you touch my knife set again, you're going to lose a fucking finger.'"

"Oh, that reminds me!" I turned to Dave, "You need to add a tally to the Hurricane Babs board."

"You're kidding me," Dave said in shock. "She hurt herself and she wasn't even in the kitchen?!"

"She sliced a finger open *during* the TV segment." I turned to Babs. "Didn't you?" I grabbed her hand and held it up.

She smiled. "Well, I wouldn't want to break the streak," which made everyone laugh as Dave walked over to the board and added a tally.

"Oh, and Jeff," Dave said with a shit-eating grin on his face, "your little *giiiirl*friend stopped by while you two were gone, and she was *not* happy that you weren't here." He and everyone else in the kitchen knew about my inappropriate arrangement with the Extortion Cougar, and they loved to give me shit about it.

The rest of the room chimed in to mock me. "*Ooooo!*" "Uh-oh!" "Someone's in *troouuble.*"

"I'll handle her," I assured them, then turned back to Emily. "Other than her, what did I miss?"

"*Bella* magazine called to ask whether your article was ready for next month, and I told them that, instead, we would be promoting a weight-loss challenge for summer; we'll get the biggest bang for our advertising buck that way." She flipped through her notebook. "Also, Sandra from the Miss Virginia organization called to say thank you; she said they received your contribution. Which reminds me, Miss Commonwealth and Miss York County called and asked whether you would help get them in shape for the Miss Virginia pageant. I booked some time for the three of you to sit down next week. And Stacey from Rotary Club called and booked you to speak in two weeks—I put it on your calendar.

"Damn, you're on it! How did I get things done before you came along?"

"You didn't," she joked as she fixed my collar.

Her phone started ringing. "Let me get this. *You* go get with your boy," she said as she pointed to Chef Kevin, "about the new menu. He promised me he'd have it done this week, but he hasn't shown me a single sample meal yet."

I walked over to Kevin, who was teaching the new guy how to make the sauces. "No, you fucking idiot; you have to sauté the garlic cloves to bring out the natural oils *before* you throw them in." . . . "No, no, jackass. First you heat the pan, then you drop the oil in, and *then* you drop the cloves in—Jesus Christ!"

"Hey, Chef," I interrupted his friendly tutorial, "what new menu items do we have for next month?"

"I came up with some shit; don't worry about it."

"That's good to hear, you cheery bastard, but Emily needs to

know what all you've got so she can promote the new meals to customers."

He let out a heavy sigh to show me how irritated he was as he
violently tossed his spatula down, then handed me a piece of paper
from his pocket. "Low-carb chicken quesadillas and sweet potato
cinnamon pinwheels—samples in the back fridge. Fuckin' happy?"

"They sound great! And how's the training going. You teaching
the new guy here how to smile and whistle while you work?" The
new guy laughed.

My cell phone buzzed with a text. "*Ah, perfect!*"

"Hey, Adam, I'm Jeff," I shook the new guy's hand. "I don't want
you to commit suicide after your first day of following Kevin around,"
I said as there was a knock at the door, "so I invited someone to visit
today so you'd see there are definitely some perks to working here."

"Come in, Diana!" I shouted, and the door swung open. Diana
Whitt was a magazine cover bikini model and Miss Swimsuit USA
Lafayette, among other titles. I had trained her for her swimsuit
competitions, and she was now using our food too. As she walked
through the door, every project in the room came to a halt. Of course,
the guys loved when she visited, but even Babs was awed by Diana's
presence. Kevin was the only one who ostensibly didn't care enough
to turn and stare.

"Diana, meet Adam," I introduced them. Adam's mouth hung
open as he shook her hand.

"Thank you so much for everything," she said to him. "I don't
know what I'd do without your food."

"Adam," I asked him, "will you let Diana taste the new menu
samples you and Kevin made?" He nodded, then nervously guided
her to the storage fridge, and before I could follow behind them,
Emily spun me around.

"Jeff! That was someone who saw your segment from earlier—
he wants us to cater his wellness event."

"Can we do it? Time, date, food?"

"Here are all the details." She handed me a yellow Post-it as both of our phones started ringing in unison. Emily stuck her finger in her ear to answer her phone as I pressed my Bluetooth.

"Hey, Manny, how's the gym doing, man? . . . Uh-huh. . . . No, you've got to reset the magnetic lock and swipe each new member's key fob to sync them up. . . ." Even though I had no official affiliation with the gym anymore, I'd made myself available to Manny ever since handing him the reins. "No problem. . . . What's that? . . . The shampoo for the men's room? Should be in the janitor's closet. . . . Yeah, that stuff kept growing legs, so I started locking it up at night. . . . Sure thing. . . . Huh? What about Libby? . . . No, don't give her a partial refund for that—*she* clogged it!" Emily started snapping her fingers at me. "Hey, Manny, I'm going to have to call you back, man. Good luck with all that."

"Hey," Emily said as she covered the phone, "I've got a customer here, Quinton something out of Georgia, saying he's lost a hundred forty pounds by eating our food!"

"That's fucking amazing! We need pics!"

"I gave him my email, and he's sending them this afternoon. Should I tell him he's going to be our customer of the month and send him his free meals?"

"No, no, we've got to give the award to Michelle L. this month; we'll make Quinton customer of the month for June."

"Why Michelle over Quinton? This guy dropped an entire person!"

"Because she was one of my original ten customers. Next month will mark thirteen straight months ordering from us and I want to thank her for it."

"Actually, that's perfect!" She got excited. "We can fly Quinton in for the Mountain Pride show!"

"Great, let's line that up." I turned to see the crowd of cooks surrounding Diana; every time she visited, morale in the kitchen always skyrocketed, but the only way to get everyone back to work was to scoot her out again quickly. "Hey D, grab a couple of those samples to take with you and let me walk you to your car."

As I guided her to the door, Emily shouted to me, "Quinton won't commit!"

I pulled up my calendar app and held it up to Diana. "Hey, do you have anything going on this weekend here? I could use some feminine help in nudging this guy she's got on the phone."

"I've got my competition in the Bahamas that weekend, remember?"

"Shit, that's right." I turned back to Emily. "You know what, that's the week after the Miss Virginia pageant, and I'll be working with the winner then. Tell Quinton that if he comes in for the show, he'll get to spend the day with Miss VA, *and* I'll take him on TV to do a segment with her too! That oughta push him over the fence."

I turned back to Diana. "All right, D, let's go out here. I need to ask you about something else." I swung the kitchen door open to find an angry-looking Extortion Cougar standing with her arms folded.

"Tell ya what; I'll call you later this afternoon, OK?" I told Diana before the Cougar shoved me back into the kitchen.

The roomful of cooks began razzing me—"Busted!" "*Ooooooo!*" "Break his legs!"—as the Cougar forcefully guided me through the kitchen toward the office.

"That's the fourth week in a row." She locked the door behind her. "That's a penalty."

"I wasn't avoiding you; I was out—"

"Save it," she said as she shoved me into my office chair and started ripping her clothes off.

About twenty minutes later, I opened the office door and did my walk of shame back into the kitchen, massaging my sore jaw as everyone laid into me.

Emily informed me, "Hey, while you were in there, Vic, the manager at Gold's Gym called. I booked you for a meeting at his gym right after lunch tomorrow."

"What does he need to meet in person for? Why can't we just talk on the phone?"

"Look, he's brought us more customers over the past three

months than all of your advertisements and news segments combined, so I suggest you go hear him out."

"Well, do you at least know what he wants to talk about?"

"All he said was that he wants to run some 'big idea' by you."

"Hey," I shouted to the front desk on the other side of the giant
warehouse-size room, "is that clock right. I had an appointment with
Vic at one fifteen?"

"Yeah," the woman behind the counter shouted back, "he's just
in there with a client; trust me, Jeff," she giggled, "he'll be done any
minute."

I nodded, then heard a deep voice barking behind me.

"What are you doing on *our* turf?" a young muscular guy in a
Gold's Gym shirt asked as he walked up and extended an open hand.

I grabbed it. "I came to show you little guys how to use those
weights over there."

He chuckled as he squeezed my arm. "You've put on some size
since you were here last." Then he turned around and shouted to
a group of guys working out in the back corner of the busy room,
"Hey! Get a load of this fucking guy!"

The three guys spun around. "Dude!" "JSP!" "What's up,
brother?!" they shouted across the gym. I waved back.

"You been using Vic's needle kit?" he asked.

"Hell no," I said as I pointed to his crotch. "I don't want to join
your teeny weenies club."

"*Fu-hu-hu-uck* you!" He laughed. "That's just a myth."

"Whatever you say, Tiny."

"So, you meeting with Vic?"

"Yeah, I guess he wants to talk about sales. You guys have been
killing it out here."

"*He* has been; he steals all our sales. Actually, I think he's in there
selling some of your food right now."

"Oh, yeah? How do you know that?"

"Well, watch." He pointed to Vic's office door. "If the client comes out with an embarrassed smile, you'll know he's just sold some of your food."

"Huh?" I asked, "What the hell does that have to do with—" Just then, the office door swung open and a blonde woman in spandex short shorts and a sports bra stepped out. She kept her smiling face pointed at the ground to avoid eye contact as she walked by us.

"See?" He bumped my arm. "There's a new customer for you."

"Jeff!" Vic's head popped out from behind the door. "Sorry about the wait, man. Come on in. Grab a seat!"

I took a chair on the opposite side of the desk from the chiseled-jawed, skin-headed ex-Marine, and couldn't help noticing the remnants of the apparent tryst that had just taken place.

"I like your shade, there." I tapped my lips then pointed to his. "What is that, fuchsia?

He wiped his mouth. "Oh, I couldn't find my lip balm this morning, so I had to borrow my wife's strawberry glitter shit, ya know?"

"Uh-huh, well, you accidentally got some of Bonnie's glitter shit on your neck there too."

He raised his hands and laughed. "What can I say?"

"So," I moved on, "what's going on, man? Was the check Emily sent to you last week too small?"

"Hell no!" he blasted. "Your check was bigger than my Gold's check last week, which is actually what I wanted to talk to you about." He waved two fingers at the door. "Shut that, will ya?" I leaned back and pushed the office door closed.

"I like working with you—the money's great and I'm selling healthy food instead of memberships that nobody uses—so I was wondering whether you'd like to officially partner up?"

"What do you mean?"

"I mean, instead of being limited to selling at Gold's, I could go gym to gym helping you replicate what I've put in place here."

"So, what, you would leave here?!"

The desk phone beeped and a woman's voice started talking, "Vic, I've got a Wendy Brown out here. She says she's your two o'clock."

"Tell her I'll be right out!" he responded, then smacked the button to hang up. "I've been hearing rumors coming down from the top that they might be trying to push me out of the picture—inner office politics and corporate bullshit!" he lightly shouted as he smacked the Gold's plaque on the wall behind him for dramatic effect. I was momentarily distracted by the neon pink thong that fell from the bookcase onto the floor as he continued on. "So I'd rather leave all this political shit behind and just work with you."

"Uh . . ." I couldn't help thinking that Bonnie, the one who had invited me to join them and their four children at their post-church family brunch last weekend, was way too conservative to be the owner of a neon pink thong. "Um, so what did you have in mind: salary, hourly, commission?"

"Straight commission, but only five percent instead of twenty."

"You don't want any base pay *and* only a quarter of what you're making now? Why the fuck would you do that?"

He pulled a manila folder from his drawer, set it on the desk, and leaned into me. "I've already got the managers at eight other gyms ready to sell your food under me." He tapped on the folder. "They'll start next week if we do this. Plus, all the trainers here are loyal to me—and to you—so the numbers won't drop here even after I leave!"

"You wily son of a bitch." I smiled. "I like the way you think."

Over the next couple of weeks the two of us formed our grassroots sales campaign. We knew we would need a few more people to help cover the lists in any reasonable amount of time. I convinced my high school buddy Roger, who had been managing a health facility down in Cocoa Beach, Florida, and Dave, who was dying to get away from the wacky chefs, to accompany me to Vic's house one evening to discuss joining our new little sales force.

When the three of us arrived, Vic already had a whiteboard loaded with bullet points and printed lists of every gym, chiropractic facility, dietitian's office, and any other business loosely associated with health in a two hundred mile radius spread across his living room table.

At first the two new guys were skeptical about this plan. "Why don't we just sell directly to the customers?" Dave asked. "Wouldn't that be easier?"

"No, this is way faster," Vic informed him, "because each new health professional we sign up already has a list of their own clients who are eagerly seeking weight-loss solutions. So each trainer, chiropractor, or dietitian we sign up to sell for us is equivalent to anywhere from twenty to a hundred or more customers."

"Yeah, but are they even allowed to sell food to people?" Roger questioned.

I interjected, "Has anyone ever told you what you can or can't sell at *your* gym?"

"Well . . . no."

"Right! Because, as you know," I said, "the health and fitness world is a *very* laissez-faire industry; there are no rules, no regulatory agencies to keep an eye on anyone, no guidelines for what you can promote and sell to customers."

"Exactly," Vic chimed back in, "health advisers, wellness coaches, and, as the four of us know, personal trainers are free to promote whatever products and services we choose: magic-pill supplements, sugary smoothies, detox programs, and, for our purposes, food."

"Dave," I asked, "how much were you making as a PT?"

"About thirty, thirty-five a year."

"Yeah, not a ton of money. But, after I introduced you to my friend Pam Sowder, and you started selling those *It Works!* weight-loss body wraps, were you not making more, some months, from those than you were from personal training?" Dave nodded in agreement.

"See my point?" I asked. "Personal trainers *need* additional products to sell in order to make a decent living. Now, Rog, how much does your gym pull in from retail?"

"About fifteen hundred a month, somewhere in that range."

I handed Roger a P&L sheet with a number circled at the bottom. "Yeah, well, this was Vic's gym's revenue—on his *worst* month."

Roger's eyes widened.

"See," I said, "as a gym operator, you want to start selling our food tomorrow, don't you?" He nodded. "But, just in case any gyms are still on the fence after seeing those numbers, you've got these." I handed Dave and him little cooler bags with some of our food samples in them, along with the sales scripts that Vic and I had created. "You just memorize and recite these scripts *exactly* as they're written," I said as the two of them choked down the samples, "and every conversation you have with a prospect will go exactly the same—guaranteed."

They both agreed.

Bonnie's head popped out from the kitchen to kindly shout, "The meat loaf's going to be done in ten minutes, so don't fill up on those food samples, boys!"

"We won't, honey!" Vic assured her.

"Now," Vic drew our attention back to the four separate stacks of paper on the table, "we'll split the locations up like this: Dave, since you're new to selling, it'll be easier to work your foot in the door at places that already sell food, so you'll take the little organic co-ops, grocery stores, and coffee-shop-type places. Roger, you'll handle places like medical weight-loss facilities and supplement retailers.

"Since I know how management works in the corporate setting," Vic continued, "I'm going to cover the big gyms and the chiropractic offices. And, Jeff, you work your magic on the personal trainers and fitness studio owners."

"I'll give it a shot."

4

SEX BRIBES

"Not so fast, *papi chulo*! You're not going anywhere yet."

I grabbed my jeans off the floor and pulled them up over my ass as I started searching the room for my shirt and shoes. One shoe was under the bed and the other somehow made its way onto the dresser, but I didn't see my shirt anywhere. I flipped over a couple of pillows on the ground, checked behind the dresser, looked to see whether it was tangled up with her pile of clothes—*nada*.

"Damn it, where's my shirt?" I asked. "Have you seen it?"

"I didn't say you could leave yet," she said as she sat upright in the bed. "*Quiero una más*."

"I know babe, but I've *gotta* hit the road."

"Well, then you better make the last one *rápida*," she said while messing with something under the covers.

"Un-*fucking*-believable!" I walked up the hall to check the living room. I searched the kitchen, the spare room, the bathroom, then returned to check the bedroom again. "Where the hell could it have gone? We never even left the room!"

"Well, you haven't checked everywhere yet," she said as she

pulled the bed cover down to reveal her bare chest. "It's always in the last place you look."

Sara thought her five-thousand-dollar E cups were her most appealing asset, but I was more turned on by her big brown eyes and her accent.

"Do you have my shirt?" I beamed.

"*Quizás*. You'll have to check for yourself," she said as a coquettish grin swept over her face.

I walked to the bed and put my hand down under the blanket and felt between her legs. Sure enough, I felt an oddly thick pair of cotton underpants on her, and I pulled the blanket back to see that she had tied my T-shirt into a pair of underwear. I tugged at it, but she wedged her butt into the mattress, pinning it down.

She wrapped her arms around my neck and said, "You'll have to fuck it off of me."

"I've gotta go, woman!"

"I'll make you a deal: you stay for fifteen more minutes and I'll make it *valer la pena*."

"Oh, it's always worth it. Believe me, babe, that's not the issue."

"No, *chico tonto*. I mean if you stay for one more round," she said, "I'll sell *twice* as much Fit Food for you this week."

After only a couple of months of partnering with her, Sara's little studio in Baltimore, Maryland, was already selling twice as much food as the other fitness studios I'd signed up, which made the regular four-hour drive to visit my friend with benefits all the more justified.

"Twice as much?! I don't know; that's pretty ambitious."

"If I can't, then I'll commute to you next time."

"Well, I like the sound of that."

"But if I *do* sell twice as much," she said as she stuck her tongue in my mouth and mumbled out the rest of her sentence, "*me deberás cuatro* next visit."

"*Four* times? That sounds like a win-win to me!" I kissed her back.

"Well," she said as she pulled her head away, "do we have a deal then, *papi*?"

I glanced at her bedside clock, "I don't *knowww* . . . I really need to get going."

She reached down and untied the shirt from her waist.

"*Deal*," I confirmed, as I started pulling my jeans back off.

In addition to sex, Sara *loved* sales quotas, and if she could up her numbers to eight grand—as she'd just suggested—I'd be sending her a weekly check for sixteen hundred dollars, in addition to the four orgasms I was now obligated to deliver.

When I returned to visit Sara the following week, she had not only hit her quota, but she'd actually beaten it.

"Not so fast, *chulo*." She stopped me from getting dressed. "You still owe me one."

"*What*?? That was four!"

"Yeah, four was if I sold eight thousand. But *vendí nueve*, so . . . " she held up all the fingers on one hand.

"Oh, come on, *five*?! I don't even know if that's going to be possible right now; you wore him out."

"I didn't say *he* had to deliver all of them. You've got hands, you've got a tongue. Be *creativo*."

"Look, how about I narrate you through number five from the road?"

She shook her head. "Business is business, *papi*." Then she signaled me over with her finger. "You agreed to the deal . . . *y ahora pagas*."

After fifteen or so minutes of some highly focused clitoral finesse, I had fulfilled my half of our new contractual obligation.

"So, tell me," I asked her as I put my shirt back on, "how did you do it?"

"*Qué?*"

"How did you sell twice as much food like it was nothing?"

"Why don't you come with me this morning and I'll show you?"

"To your gym?"

"*Sí!*" She got excited. "Spend a couple of hours there! My clients have been dying to meet you."

She had an amazing little gym, more like a CrossFit box, really—no machines, no equipment other than a handful of bands, medicine balls, a couple of boxes for jumping, a row of kettlebells, and a dozen dumbbells, none of which exceeded fifteen pounds. The workouts were by appointment only, and because she didn't charge membership—the number one revenue source for most gyms—she relied heavily on selling retail, which was why the area by the front door was jam-packed with protein bars and powder, water bottles, smoothies, a plethora of healthy little snacks, and a minifridge that she had lined with my meals.

Typically, our customers paid for all their food up front and then we shipped it to their homes, one and done. But Sara had uncovered an interesting psychological glitch in the way people thought about buying: yes, you can ask someone to spend a hundred and fifty bucks all at once for their food, but if you ask them to do it five dollars at a time, spread throughout the week, they'll end up spending two hundred without even realizing it. So, without even trying, Sara had gotten the same number of customers to spend more money on food.

Also, by having the meals on-site, Sara brought in tons of new foot traffic to her studio—proprietors from surrounding businesses would stop in and grab lunch, drivers-by who saw the carb-free pizza poster she hung in the window popped in to try it, and gym members would bring their coworkers in to try a peanut butter protein brownie who would then walk out the door with a handful of them. And although customers were buying more food now, they were actually spending less money. Shipping a single order of food required a two-inch-thick Styrofoam cooler (fifteen dollars), roughly ten pounds of dry ice depending on the time of year and which state we were shipping to (another fifteen dollars), and the FedEx charges (twenty dollars). All in all, it cost about two grand to ship forty customer orders. So, by shipping all the food to one location, the cost per meal dropped by almost a dollar fifty. And my favorite part was that, since the customers were now paying Sara for their food instead of me, I didn't have to track each order and send her a commission check at the end of the week or month.

I locked myself in Sara's office and called Vic to tell him the news.

"Are you serious?"

"Yep."

"The FedEx bill dropped *that* much?

"Yep."

"So her sales doubled in one week and the customers actually paid less?!"

"Uh-huh."

"And you're saying you don't have to track her commissions *or* send her a check each week?"

"That's right."

"So the gyms buy it wholesale, mark it up to retail price, and then just pocket the difference?"

"Yep."

"And you know her clients will never let her stop ordering the food now; if she ever runs out, they'll bitch until she orders more."

"You got that right!"

"I think I've got an idea."

Vic owned and hosted the annual Mountain Pride Championship in Virginia, a nationals-qualifying bodybuilding competition that drew some of the biggest names in fitness, along with thousands of gym owners and aspiring personal trainers.

"You know, we should mention this wholesaling thing at the Championship this weekend," he said. "Why don't *you* do the success story presentation at the end of the show—you can pitch one time, and the food will be in like a thousand gyms by next week!"

"Nah, man. You need to do it; you're the sales king."

"We'll do a one-two punch. You can sell from the stage better than me, then I'll catch them with the face-to-face afterward to collect their checks. Can you head back to Roanoke tonight? We'll need to get everything set up for you first thing in the morning"

"I'll leave this evening."

—

I was exhausted by the time I got back from Sara's place in Baltimore. It was close to midnight when I tossed my briefcase in the direction of the coffee table and collapsed onto the couch. As soon as I drifted off to sleep, I was jolted back into my living room by a loud banging at my front door.

I staggered to the door and looked through the peephole to see an angry-looking Extortion Cougar staring right back at me.

"I know you're in there," she said. "Now open this door so you can catch up on payments." I stayed still in fear that she might hear a creak on the floor if I moved. After a couple of minutes of banging and demanding that I open the door, everything went silent. I checked the peephole—no Cougar.

When my heart stopped pounding, I tiptoed over to the couch and laid down. Just when I was drifting back into that fuzzy place between the real world and the dream world, my phone buzzed twice—it was no longer being charged. The entire room had gone dark. A fuse had blown.

I contemplated ignoring it, since the fuse boxes for the entire building were in the main hallway, but then I remembered the food samples in the fridge for the show tomorrow.

I walked down the hall and flipped the fuse switch, then stumbled back to my unit. As I closed the door, the Cougar appeared. My heart leapt into my throat.

She didn't say anything as she unbuttoned her long black coat to reveal her fully naked body underneath it. She dropped the jacket to the floor and started backing me into the couch. She shoved me onto my back and leapt on top of me, pinning my arms down with her knees, and started unzipping my pants. I was painfully tired, but it was pointless to attempt reasoning with her.

"If I'm going to miss out on sleep anyway," I thought to myself as I felt the Cougar's cold little hands make their way through my zipper, "I may as well enjoy it."

5

QUINTON LOST 140 POUNDS, "AND SO CAN YOU!"

I walked backstage into the coed prep area to get ready to take the stage for my presentation. There were naked bodies—men and women—standing all around me and applying last-minute spray tan and glue to hold their suits to their skin. A tit falling out of a bikini top here, a ball dangling from a Speedo there—no one cared. They just applied some glue, tucked the body part in, and kept going. A group of them were huddled in a circle drinking wine; this was an old but common practice at bodybuilding shows, originally used as a diuretic to excrete water and bring out your veins to make you look more muscular. Now that we know asparagus does the same thing, the wine is mostly used to calm the competitors' nerves before stepping out in front of a crowd of thousands wearing nothing but expensive lingerie.

When I heard my name over the speaker system, I snapped into performance mode. After Vic introduced me, I walked to the front of the stage followed by my Vanna White-ish assistant and three average-looking individuals whom I invited from behind the curtain to come out and join me. As they walked past me to center stage and stood in front of the three easels that were each holding a giant blank poster board, I began explaining who these individuals were and why they were there.

"On your right," I addressed the audience, "is a gentleman I just met for the first time in person yesterday. Ladies and gentlemen, this is Quinton, who traveled all the way from Atlanta, Georgia, to stand on this stage tonight and share his accomplishment with all of us. You see, six months ago, this was Quinton." My lovely Vanna look-alike walked over and flipped the poster board to reveal Quinton's before picture. "But standing before you today is a vibrant, energetic one-hundred-and-forty-pound-lighter man—no!—*warrior*." The crowd started clapping wildly. "Who took control of his life and made the amazing change you see in front of you!" Then Quinton signaled that he wanted to say something into the mic.

"I couldn't have done it without Fit Food," he said. "And I know that if I can do it, anyone out there can do it!"

When the crowd finally settled down, I stepped to the other side of Quinton and put my hand on the next man's shoulder. "Next I want you all to meet Greg. This man is without a doubt one of the biggest winners to walk across this stage tonight. The reason Greg deserves a thunderous applause from you guys is because he did this." Vanna revealed his before picture and I let the crowd rumble for a minute. "Now, Greg, I'm sure everyone here wants to know how it must feel to have lost ninety-nine pounds and become the stud we see standing before us now." And then I held the mic up to him.

"Jeff, this was by far the hardest thing I've ever done, but it was worth the fight because I feel," he said as he pointed at Vanna, "as good as your assistant looks!" The crowd chuckled, then he continued: "And I can't let this go unsaid: I owe it all to Fit Food. You guys helped me change my life. My daughter can actually get her arms all the way around me now when she hugs her papa." Once again, I let the crowd roar for a minute before I raised my hand to settle them back down.

"Now, that was a pretty good applause," I said to the audience, "but, let me tell ya, what you're about to learn is going to make you blow the fucking roof off." As everyone leaned forward in their seat, I thought I heard a pin drop.

"Now there's no doubt Greg looks phenomenal. The thing you can't see about Greg, however, is his bigger victory. Not long ago, he was facing a very dark and powerful opponent, an opponent who had backed him into a corner and beaten him within an inch of his life. But Greg said, '*No!* I refuse to go out this way,' and he looked deep within himself, mustered up every single ounce of might that he possessed, and through patience and determination, Greg willpowered the reversal," I said as I grabbed his hand and raised it straight into the air, "of his *type 2 diabeteees!*"

A wave of *woo-hoos* clashed with feet stomping and hands banging together at violent speeds in celebration of Greg's glorious achievement. His eyes watered up and his grin stretched ear to ear.

Then I walked to the front of stage and held my hand up again, and after a couple of seconds, the crowd grew silent.

"Last but not least," I continued, "standing on your far left is a very special lady. You can call her Ronda. But I've always referred to her as 'Mom.'" A predictable *awww* came from the crowd. "Now, as I'm about to share with you the success of this person who's so special to me," I said as I pointed out to the audience, "I want you to take one second to think about that special person in *your* life—that person whom you'd like to see standing up on this stage beside a picture of his or her former self. Someone you know who's been struggling for years: Your mom. Your dad. Your best friend. Your client."

I stood silent for a second staring out at the sea of glassy eyes in front of me, each one visualizing that special someone.

"I want you to come up to me after the show and tell me about your special person, and let me tell you from experience, the greatest feeling in the world isn't even knowing that you helped your loved one make an *amazing* fifty-pound transformation." I swung my arm back to Vanna, who revealed my mother's before picture. A few hoots and whistles escaped from the crowd. *"Not even close!"*

"The greatest feeling in the world comes when you look at that special someone in your life," I said as I pointed to my mother's face, "and you see that right there." She was smiling so big, it looked like it hurt. *"That's* the greatest feeling in the world." I threw my arms out wide, *"I love you so much, Mom!"*

The room exploded as everyone rose for a standing ovation. I walked over and hugged her, and the crowd refused to sit down for what felt like the most wonderful eternity. I wished it would never end.

6

LEARNING FROM THE MASTER: MCDONALD'S

The following weekend, I owed Sara five orgasms, two of which were still pending when my phone woke us up on Monday morning. When she saw Emily's name on the screen, she knew it was business and tried to pull the ringing phone from my hand.

"Babe, please!" I pleaded. "I gotta take this call."

I wrestled it from her and swiped the screen. "Hey, Emily," I said excitedly, "what an amazing week, huh?" Sara started massaging me under the covers.

"Jeff! You need to get over here right away," Emily shouted over some arguing voices in the background.

"Hey, Emily, I—Sara, stop! Em, I can barely hear you."

"People are furious! My phone has been lighting up all morning from gym owners and customers calling to complain about their orders."

"What's wrong?" I rolled on my side in an attempt to take my focus off of Sara's roaming hands.

"A lot of their food showed up spoiled—the meals delivered to the West Coast sat in the heat for too long and the dry ice melted; some packages were even busted open."

"Oh, shit!"

"That's not all. Our longtime customers are complaining that their favorite meals taste different than usual, and, get this, a lot of customers said they aren't losing weight on the program—too many to be a coincidence—and now all of these people want refunds, and I don't know what to tell them. It's fucking chaos over here!"

"How the hell did so many things go wrong overnight?"

"I don't know, but if we don't find a way to fix this we're going to lose all the new customers we just signed up!"

"OK, OK, well, we'll just send the gyms replacement packages with a—" The arguing voices in the background were getting louder "Emily, what the hell is going on over there?"

"It's Babs and Kevin; they won't stop fighting."

Once Sara had gotten me aroused, she lifted the blanket and climbed onto my lap. "Can you move Babs to a different project, so they're not working together?"

"It won't matter; he's picking fights with everyone. And Babs's getting worse too; the other day I walked into the kitchen and," she turned her voice to a loud whisper, "and her crazy ass was cleaning the inside of one of the ovens *while* slow-roasting a tenderloin in it."

"OK, Emily, I'll—*mmm!* I'll talk to her—*mmm!*" I had to keep shifting my face side to side to escape Sara's tongue trying to force its way into my mouth.

"You need to get down here!"

"I can't—*mmm!* Can't right now—*mm-mmm!*" I put my hand over Sara's face. "I've got sales meetings with new studios all afternoon."

"So what do you want to do about the West Coast replacements? If we send them more food, it's just going to show up ruined again."

"Well, maybe we can—"

"And," Emily cut me off, "what am I supposed to tell the customers? *I* don't know why they're not losing weight! That's your department. I need you back in the kitchen!"

"But—"

"I'm not asking; I'm telling you."

The next morning, I got to the kitchen an hour before anyone else, so that I would have a chance to inspect the scene before getting sucked into the daily fray, but instead, I found Babs bent over the giant cutting table, wailing into her hands. I put my hand on her back. "Babs, What's wrong?"

A mixture of tears and saliva hung from her lips as she lifted her head and spewed at me, "My boyfriend broke up with me. My life is over!"

In astonishment, I blurted, "*You* had a boyfriend?!" Then quickly I tried to recover. "I mean—I'm sorry. I promise it's going to be OK." I picked up her cell phone off the table and held it out. "Do you want to call someone—a friend, your brother?"

She wiped her sniffling nose and asked, "Can I talk with you?"

"Oh, sure," I said with trepidation, "I just don't know how helpful I'll be at relationship advice."

"You're good at solving problems." She wiped her eyes and chin.

"OK, well, what happened?"

"Chip thinks I'm a klutz, who breaks everything I touch. He said I'm too exhausting, and that he can't talk to me anymore."

"Hey, if he can't appreciate you for you," I said, "you don't want to be with him anyway, right? There's a great guy out there looking for you right now."

"No, I'm not upset about that," she whined.

"Well, why are you upset then?"

She started crying again. "I just gave him a brand-new iPad."

"I see. Well, yeah, that sucks, but it's just a couple of hundred bucks right?"

"Five hundred!" she shouted.

"OK, but, come on, it's not the end of the world." I downplayed her loss. "So you're out five hundred bucks."

"No, you don't understand. Chip only told me about his birthday the day before, and I couldn't get him a present because my cards are all maxed out, so I took out a loan."

"You took out a loan to buy an iPad?" I asked.

"Well, no, not at first," she justified. "I got the loan to pay down my credit cards, but then I panicked when he told me it was his birthday; I wanted to impress him."

"Why the hell would you take out another loan to pay off cre—" I stopped myself, "Uh, well, do you want to call and ask him for the iPad back, so you can return it and get your money?"

After letting out a frustrated moan she continued, "I already tried. He won't answer my calls."

"OK, what are you going to do, then?"

She wiped her nose again and looked up at me with her pouty blue eyes. "Well, if you could lend me the money, I promise I'd pay you back fast."

"Babs, I think that . . . well, the best thing to—"

"You don't understand," she interjected. "I can't default on this loan. They'll start taking all my stuff away!"

"But, Babs," I tried to reason with her, "me giving you the money isn't going to help you."

In desperation she came back with "I know it's a lot of money, but I'll make it up. I'll do anything you want: I'll work extra, I'll stay late, anything."

"But, Babs, there's not really any extra work to do."

"I'll do *anything*! You name it!"

"I don't know. I can't think of anyth—" Before I could finish my sentence, she crossed her arms, grabbed the bottom of her shirt with both hands, and lifted it straight over her head, then dropped it at her feet.

"Babs, listen, I don't think—" "Wow, those are nicer than I thought they'd be," I thought to myself. "Uh, I don't think that's such a good idea. You work for me."

"Anything you want, I'll do it," she said, batting her eyes at me.

"And I appreciate that," I said, as I struggled to ward off the movie reel of sexual scenarios playing through my mind. "It's . . . it's just not the smart thing to do," I said out loud to myself.

She started rubbing her hands over her breasts. "Just tell me what you want me to do. Just name it!"

I suppose that, from witnessing how submissive I was with the Extortion Cougar, Babs had learned how to play to my weakness. She'd trapped me in an awkward situation.

I stepped up to her and, to *my* surprise, said, "Babs. More than anything, I want you to stop taking out bank loans." Then I leaned down and grabbed her shirt, and smiled as I handed it back to her, which made her smile too.

"You're an amazing woman and all," I said, "but if I cross this line with you, that means I've got to sleep with all my employees, and there's no way I'm fucking Casey!"

"Put this on, damn it," I said, and forced the shirt into her hand.

"Well," she asked, fully clothed again, and now in a lighter mood, "Any idea of what I should do?"

"Your ex," I pulled out my phone to open Google Maps, "where does he work?"

"At that Remax right up the road."

"Perfect. Why don't you give me his card and I'll swing by there this afternoon and see about getting the iPad back? And, in the meantime," I said as I winked at her, "keep your shirt on," which made her chuckle again.

In an attempt to put her misappropriated loyalty to good use, I gave her a mission. "I'll tell you what you *can* do for me, though. Lately, we've had a number of customers complaining that they're not losing weight on the program, and some complaints about the taste of some of our meals. Can you keep an eye open and see if you can find any funny business going on in here for me?"

"I'll do it!" she saluted.

It didn't take her more than an hour into the day's shift to discover the problem and report back to me. Apparently, Kevin had gotten bored with the current menu and began ignoring my nutritional guidelines so that he could create better-tasting recipes. She sneak-ily snapped videos of him putting starch in the cinnamon porridge, bread crumbs in the tuna cakes, pure sugar and extra salt in the to-mato sauce, and dribbling melted butter on everything.

Then she noticed that the cooks hadn't been weighing out every single meal, which was throwing off the portion sizes. Not only was this affecting the customers' results, but it was messing up our bot-tom line because Emily couldn't run a proper P&L sheet if they didn't weigh every meal down to the ounce to give her an accurate food cost.

And the one who annoyed me most of all, of course, was Casey.

Babs discovered that he had been inventing his own recipes and sneaking them into the customers' packages in place of the ones they had ordered. Some customers had ordered our turkey meatballs; Casey replaced them with a serving of his five-alarm chili. A few of the customers who'd been expecting our burger patties instead got Casey's Southern meat loaf recipe. And the poor souls hoping to try our famous Carolina-style pulled pork instead received Casey's new Italian sausage gumbo. His meals all sounded amazing, actually, but that wasn't the point—it was that nobody knew they existed. Kevin didn't approve them, Emily didn't have any budget set aside for them, I had no clue of whether they met the nutritional guidelines, and, of course, since they weren't on the menu, customers didn't know they were ordering them.

I felt like throwing a hair-pulling temper tantrum, deducting what they were costing me from their checks, and then firing Casey as a cherry on top, but I decided I wouldn't say anything until I'd cooled my head. There was a McDonald's right down the road, so I would go grab a cup of joe while I decided how to address the situation.

I was sitting in the booth with my cup of coffee, stewing over the sloppy, irresponsible mess I'd allowed the kitchen to become.

Then something at the McDonald's counter caught my attention. Every time a customer walked up and placed an order, the employees repeated the same motions, in unison with each other, at a lethargic yet efficient movement and pace. I knew McDonald's didn't typically hire the most highly skilled Harvard grad engineers as their staff, and yet, the speed, efficiency, and consistency that these employees were using was astounding.

As I watched them in motion, I wasn't watching employees working at a fast-food restaurant; all I saw were patterns, motion rituals, and conditioned procedures. They looked like robots as they moved about their kitchen. Every single thing had a place and a process, so that every customer order resulted in a choreographed action.

It was beautiful.

After a few minutes, I walked up to the counter and asked to speak with the owner. I asked her, as a fellow kitchen owner, how she was able to get her staff to work so methodically and consistently. She went to the back and returned with a fat binder full of papers.

"This is our operation manual," she said as she flipped open to a random page. "Every McDonald's has one. There's a detailed procedure for every single thing we do, and each task is so small and broken down into mechanical steps, a crew member would have to put in *extra* effort to mess it up—which, trust me, *ain't* gonna happen."

I asked if she wouldn't mind letting me sit at the booth and take a look at it for a few minutes. "And here," I said as I pulled my wallet out from my pocket, "you can hold on to this until I bring the manual back."

"*Weeeell* . . . You don't own a Wendy's or a Burger King, do ya?"

"No," I chuckled, "I'm not competition for you; it's a healthy meal delivery company."

"Oh, just like Nutrisystem!"

"No, we're *not* ju—" I sighed. "Yeah . . . like Nutrisystem."

She happily handed it over.

As I started to skim through it, I couldn't believe how minutely specific every single task was. Each person had a specific place to stand based on the task he or she was performing, and each movement had a time assigned to it, so that they could assure that each order took no more than forty-five seconds to produce. The burger assembly procedure, for example, was shared by three cooks: cook number one toasts bread products at five hundred forty-five degrees and grabs a paper wrapper for it to be placed on (eleven seconds); cook number two grabs the condiments, which are kept at room temperature, so they don't chill the sandwich, and after cook number one finishes toasting the bun, grabs the preheated meat product, and places it on the bread (twenty seconds); cook number three adds condiments on top of the meat patty, wraps the food, and sends it to a heated landing pad (fourteen seconds). They even had a detailed procedure for *exactly* how to place the condiments on the patty, so that when customers bit into their sandwiches, a pickle wouldn't shoot out into their laps.

How ingenious!

So, this was McDonald's secret; this was how they made sure that each location produced the same result in the same amount of time, for every customer, every day. The reason my cooks were messing things up wasn't because they were incompetent—at least no more so than any McDonald's staff member—they just didn't have specific systems and procedures to follow. The goal was to use minimally skilled employees so that I wouldn't have to rely on talents, motivation, or personality traits, and then give them simple tasks like assembly line workers.

I'd witnessed a lot of entrepreneur friends ambitiously start a business, only to find themselves stuck a few years into it—unable to break free from the frustrating hustle and bustle of running a mom-and-pop business—and transition to being hands-off business owners. And I'd just realized what all of us had been missing: business systems. It made perfect sense, because having a system for every little thing was the only way to ensure consistency and, therefore, exponential growth.

I snapped shots of as many pages as I could, traded the manual back for my wallet, and headed to the kitchen to begin writing an operation manual of my own.

7

MERLOT: THE BREAKFAST OF CHAMPIONS

Later that night, I took Emily, Dave, and Vic out to my favorite pub to split a couple of pitchers of green beer for Saint Paddy's Day. We were laughing our asses off as we took turns sharing stories of the chefs' wacky hijinks. Vic was describing Babs's latest mishap—she had approached Kevin in the middle supergluing a broken spider ladle, and grabbed it out of his hand to clean it at which point it became superglued to her hand—while animatedly impersonating Hurricane Babs trying to pry the ladle from her skin with a steak knife.

In the middle of his story, my attention was hijacked by the stunning blonde goddess walking through the front door. Everything else in the room disappeared. When she caught my gaze, it was obvious we both felt the energy.

I walked over to her.

"Hey, I didn't mean to pull you away from your girlfriends," I said, with my eyes still locked onto her giant baby blues, "but I noticed you challenging me to a staring contest, and I can't let you win without a fight."

She smiled the most beautiful smile in the world.

"I'm Jeff," I said as I extended my hand.

She ran her fingers across her forehead, pulling her bleach-blonde hair out of her face and wrapping it behind her ear. "I'm Brie." She grabbed my hand and didn't let go.

We took the last two seats at the edge of the bar, and she ordered some vodka-loaded mixed drink. I told the bartender to "make it two."

At first, I struggled to focus on her words; I was too busy obsessing over every little detail of her face. She had this adorable dent in the middle of her nose—it was broken as a child, she told me, when her older sister hit her square in the face with a baseball bat—she was self-conscious about it, but I thought it made her beauty even more distinct.

While she was talking, I was mesmerized by the sexy little Georgia May Jagger–style gap between her two front teeth—every now and then she would stick the tip of her tongue through it after taking a sip of her drink. It was driving me crazy!

We were both born in Roanoke, salespeople, big into fitness and nutrition, extroverted socialites, read books and hated reality TV, not religious, politically engaged, shared the same views, and radiated self-confidence.

"So, you're in sales—what kind?"

"Well, I'm looking to get into pharmaceuticals—it's such a rapidly growing market—but, at the moment, I sell spirits."

"You're kidding me. What a wild coincidence . . ."

"What?" she eagerly asked.

"I *buy* spirits!"

As she laughed, she rested her hand on my leg. Time stopped for a minute.

"Did you just say your father is Roy Nelson?"

"That's right." She smiled almost as if she had been testing to see whether I'd be afraid.

"Roanoke Roy?" I asked in disbelief. "The Cavespring Brawler?

The Roy Nelson who beat the shit out of that cop in public, then threw a Molotov cocktail into his car?"

"The police chief was so afraid of him, they never even chased him," she said proudly. Nine out of ten guys would get up from the table and sprint away if they realized they were flirting with Roy Nelson's youngest daughter, so I would dare to do the polar opposite.

"He's a legend around here. You've got to introduce me to him!"

She locked onto my eyes and said, "OK."

We must have sat talking for hours, because when I turned to show her my crew, they had all left, and the same was true of her girlfriends. At the end of the night, I walked her across the parking lot, and when we got to her car, I stuck my tongue out at her, asking, "Did the drinks make my tongue green?"

She laughed as I showed it to her. Then she asked, "How about mine?" And as she stuck her long, green tongue out at me, I couldn't resist. I wrapped my lips around it and tried sucking it right out of her mouth. She pulled me into her, mashing us up against the side of her car, right there in the middle of the busy parking lot.

I'd never felt anything like this before.

Over the next few weeks, Brie started swinging by the kitchen around lunchtime each day to visit me, and without being asked, she would dive right in and help with whatever project I was working on. I loved having her in the kitchen, just her presence made me work faster. When she left, I always sent her on her way with her favorite Fit Food lunch—tuna cake with spicy buffalo sauce on top—and an extra one so she would have something to eat for dinner. She was my favorite thing; she was what I looked forward to each day.

I was on a mission to create my operations manual as quickly as I could, so that my business would run on autopilot without me having to worry about everything falling apart. I threw myself into the kitchen completely.

Emily flipped the light on as she walked into my office and popped her head over my laptop. "Did you sleep here again last night?"

"Why would you think that?" I said as I kept typing away.

"The bags under your eyes are a start, and you're wearing the same shirt as yesterday."

"Yeah, well," I said before I stopped to down the last sip of my Big Gulp, "there was no point in going home for four hours just to turn around and come right back."

She walked around to see what I was working on. "What's so important you couldn't stop to go home and sleep? 'If sheet one AF12 is less than or equal to sheet two J27, then divide by eighteen times three and a half plus sheet two M8 divided by eighty-eight'—what the hell is this gibberish?"

"It's an algorithm. Hold on." I kept typing away. "You're making me lose my train of thought."

"I think you're losing your mind."

"*Aaaaaand* got it!"

"Got what?"

"Check it out." I stood up and offered my seat to her. "Pull up today's orders, just like you normally would, and then copy and paste them right here."

While she pulled up her files, I took my Big Gulp cup over to the Keurig and popped in a Starbucks K-cup. When it finished, I glanced over at Emily, who was reading today's orders aloud as she entered them into the spreadsheet—"430 mango chicken, 225 fajita steak, 290 turkey pinwheels, 103 teriyaki chicken, 342 fiesta fatata, 415 turkey meat loaf with laban sauce." I made sure Emily wasn't paying attention to me as I grabbed one of the 750 ml bottles of cheap red that Kevin used to test new sauces with and diluted my coffee down to a fifty-fifty mixture of Pike Place blend and Yellow Tail merlot—my second so far this morning.

"Oh, my god!" she said. "This is unbelievable."

"Pretty cool, huh? This means we don't have to rely on Cryin' Kevin to do our inventory and grocery order forms anymore. You just input our current inventory in this column here, along with each day's order totals in this one here, and the spreadsheet will calculate the grocery lists. Then all you have to do is fax them over to the purveyors and they'll pull everything together."

I grabbed one of the lists fresh off the printer and handed it to her.

Seventy-four lbs of ground beef at $2.84/lb	Total: $210.16
Six boxes of 8 oz containers at $34.18/box	Total: $205.08
Ninety-two lbs of chicken breast at $1.97/lb	Total: $181.24
Seventeen lbs of salmon at $8.87/lb	Total: $150.79
Ten cans of tuna at $9.58/can	Total: $95.80
Eight 5 lb packs of ground turkey at $11.55/pack	Total: $92.40
Two boxes of 16 oz containers at $34.82/box	Total: $69.64
Eight bundles of asparagus at $5.98/bundle	Total: $47.84
Nine thirty-six packs of eggs at $4.42/each	Total: $39.78
Five 2 lb packs of green beans at $5.98/pack	Total: $29.90
Six pts of Greek yogurt at $3.39/ea	Total: $20.34
Three oz of fresh dill at $2.64/oz	Total: $7.92
Two containers of crumbled blue cheese at $2.98/pack	Total: $5.96
Two oz of fresh mint leaves at $2.61/oz	Total: $5.22
Two 8 oz packages of mushrooms at $1.97/pack	Total: $3.94
	Grand Total: $1,166.01

"This is amazing. How did you get all these prices?"

I'd entered the entire US Foods catalog into the spreadsheet, and then spent the previous night running through the aisles at Sam's Club writing down the price per unit for every single item in the store—a nervous employee followed me the entire time, asking me who I was working for—and then came back to the kitchen and plugged them into the algorithms.

I took a giant swig of my drink. "All that matters is it's done!"

She spun around in her chair to face me. "Well, I'm worried about you; you're practically living in the kitchen now, and it's killing you."

"I'm fine," I tried to assure her.

"You look like a crippled zombie—you're not even standing up straight—and you're so stressed and intense lately. It's OK to ask for help, you know."

"Seriously, I'm good."

"Talk to me. What's wrong?"

What was I supposed to say? Yeah, my knees hurt because I was rarely sitting down. My back was killing me because I was constantly leaning over a table dicing, mixing, or measuring something. I was exhausted from wearing so many different hats—cook, manager, bookkeeper, and head of human resources, sales, marketing, and, my least favorite, customer service.

"Thank you for calling Fit Food. This is Jeff. How can I help you?" . . . "Yes, Jeff from TV—what can I do for you?" . . . "Yes, ma'am, we'll deliver it right to your door." . . . "No, we're *not* just like Nutrisystem. Our food tastes good, and you'll *actually* lose weight."

What did Emily want to hear? That I was stressed because I was falling behind on my regular duties? That the articles I had to write for two different magazines were both behind schedule? That my speeches were suffering because I didn't have time to prepare? Would it have helped if I had whined about how horrible I was at keeping the books—and complained about how the receipts, invoices, checkbook, and payroll were getting backed up? I could easily have bitched about the fact that managing the shipping logistics for perishable products was a fucking nightmare and a package of food would sporadically show up spoiled—or sometimes not at all—or that the Extortion Cougar was constantly trying to hunt me down for payments, but with Brie in the picture now, I was always scuttling to avoid her, or about the chefs—*my god*, the chefs—were such completely different animals than the normal employees I was used to.

Here I was, in my midtwenties, babysitting adults ten, twenty, thirty years older than I who acted like children and made me want to pull my fucking hair out.

"Nah, I'm good," I answered Emily, then took another gulp.

"You'd be a better liar if you didn't wear your emotions on your face. And I know this," she said smiling, "because, for a guy who spends so much time on his appearance, you look like shit." Then she closed the door and left me in peace.

I downed the last of my drink, filled my mug with another round, and went back to work on my systems.

Things went on like this for months as I continued designing, testing, and then training everyone on the new processes.

Each of these systems had to be designed so that any person could carry them out regardless of personal attributes—tall, short, strong, weak, introverted, extroverted, fast, slow, ambitious, lethargic. If I found myself using my hand strength to open an olive jar, I stopped, scratched out that process, and rewrote it so that the magnetic opener was the new technique. When I caught myself veering from my sales script and improvising to smooth-talk a gym owner into selling our food, I either wrote down the new line as protocol or nixed it and got back to my script.

Instead of lifting up the thirty-five pound drum of oil to pour it into the fryer like I normally would, I stuck a tube into the bottom so the fryer could be refilled without anyone having to attempt lifting the oil drum over his or her head. When I caught myself speeding up to get a task done quicker, I purposely slowed myself down so I could document a pace and time in which an employee would realistically be able to perform the task. Once I had discovered the most efficient procedure for each task, I would then corral Emily, the sales guys, and the chefs, and rehearse, rehearse, and *rehearse* ad nauseam, until every little process was completely robotic.

It was around midnight on a Thursday when I'd finally gotten my operations manual completed. The systems were written down to the most infinitesimal detail, just like McDonald's, and everyone had been trained on them. After living in the kitchen for months, exhausted, stressed, and slightly buzzed, it was now time to see whether the systems would all work in my absence.

8

TAKING ON INVESTORS: LET THE REAL FRAUD BEGIN

I slept in the next day, not because I wanted to, but because it was the first time I hadn't slept on a floor in weeks and I was so mentally and physically drained. Instead of going straight to the kitchen, I took Brie to brunch, where we had crab omelets and mimosas, and sat for hours catching up on life outside the kitchen. After brunch, she talked me into joining her for a pedicure, which I fought all the way to the spa, until she recruited the entire staff to force me into the chair. When the little Asian woman first laid her hands on my feet, however, I shut up. Brie sat in the chair beside me taking pictures and giggling at me. This was the most relaxing Friday I'd had since I had started my company over two years before. I felt guilty.

Around noon, Brie and I drove up to the Roanoke Star, the ninety-foot-tall fluorescent star on top of Mill Mountain that overlooks the city. As we stood there, watching the cars scrambling all over the city below us, I felt myself getting anxious. I couldn't get the kitchen out of my head—what if an operation had gone completely awry?

"Hey," I asked Brie, "do you think Emily will remember to book FedEx Express for Monday and hold all the West Coast orders so they don't sit in the warehouse over the weekend?"

"Baby," she consoled me as kindly as she could, "Emily has everything taken care of. You need to relax."

"OK, but what about the sales guys? Dave's got a meeting with a huge potential client today. What if he goes off script and botches the whole deal?"

"Let me see your phone," she politely demanded.

I thought she might toss it off the mountain, but I took the gamble and handed it to her anyway.

She spun her thumb around the screen for a few seconds. "Here," she said as she turned to show me. "Here's the FedEx app. You can log in like this and see all your deliveries—when they're scheduled to be picked up, where they're in transit, and you can even set it to alert you when they've arrived. And, see, Emily booked Express for Monday, just like you asked!" Then she opened another app. "And here's Wells Fargo. Looks like Vic just signed up a new account. See here? Seventy-two hundred dollars is pending from a place called Balance Chiropractic. And look here: there's a pending transaction for a place called Fitness Revolution. Is that the one Dave's working on?"

"Holy shit! The scripts worked for him!"

"See? Everything's under control, baby. You worked hard to build this. You should enjoy it."

"Thanks, princess." I put the phone away and wrapped my arm around her. I did my best to be present with Brie throughout the afternoon, but every half hour or so, I would impulsively check the apps to ease my nerves. Around five o'clock, I couldn't take it anymore and decided to head over to the kitchen.

I walked through the door to hear AC/DC's "Back in Black" blasting through the speakers as the circus of chefs danced around each other singing along with Bon Scott. "Wow, the original version! Why did that asshole have to go and die of alcohol poisoning?!" I thought. Suddenly, I didn't want to think about that anymore.

There was a pungent garlic aroma and some sort of pirogue mushroom concoction sizzling in the frying pans, and in the center of the room, the four-by-eight aluminum table was covered with a beautiful spread of meals, each one identical to the one next to it—a colorful veggie medley paired with a lightly seasoned and seared ahi steak.

I walked over to Emily. "Hey, isn't all this stuff being made a little late in the day; I mean, won't the delivery truck be pulling up anytime now?"

"He came and picked everything up about an hour ago; we got done early, so I thought I'd have them get a jump start on tomorrow's work."

"Get the fuck outta here!" I said in disbelief.

"Also, your little girlfriend stopped by about an hour ago. She wasn't happy that you weren't here, again."

"Brie? I've been with her all day."

"No, your *other* girlfriend. Does Brie even know about her?"

"There's nothing to *know*."

"I doubt you two were going into your office to chat."

"When was the last time you saw us go into the office? I've been avoiding the Cougs on purpose—that's why she's pissed."

"Why don't you just tell her to fuck off? Or better yet, tell Brie about her and I *know* she'll tell her to fuck off!"

"I want to, *believe* me, but I can't. This building isn't up to code, and she's the only thing keeping us from being shut down. I'm not sleeping with her anymore—even though she's trying!—but, ironically, we need her. If Brie gets in her face, we'll lose everything, so if you like working here, you've got to keep your mouth shut, OK?"

"OK, OK! Hey, do me a favor and check the calendar app on your phone; I want to make sure everything synced up correctly." I tapped the app and handed her the phone. "All right, good! See. here?" She showed me. "All the sales guys' daily agendas will show up here from now on—you can see their scheduled appointments, whom they're with, how the meeting went, and all the contact information, just in case you need it. Oh, that reminds me: have you talked with Dave yet?"

"No, but I saw he had some transaction pending in the account. I guess that means his meeting went well!"

"So you haven't heard about the Fitness Revolution guys?"

"No, other than he apparently signed them up to sell for us. Why? What's the deal?"

"You need to call Dave."

"Just tell me. Is it good news? Bad news?"

"Call him."

"OK, I'll call him in just a few."

Looking around my kitchen, I was awed. It was hard to believe that these people—*my* wacky chefs—were gliding swiftly around their workspace, just as I'd seen the McDonald's employees do.

The cooks finished sealing the last of the ahi meals and cleaned the countertops as Emily packed up her laptop. She gave me a high five behind the chefs on her way out the door, and I was left standing in a clean, empty kitchen. It was hard to believe that the stressful chaos I'd been swimming through just days ago turned into this one hundred percent choreographed show.

I felt my head getting heavy as a mixture of serotonin, dopamine, and endorphins swirled around each other. I collapsed onto the office floor, partly from mental exhaustion and partly from relief. I was filled with an intense sense of accomplishment. After having lived in this prison of a kitchen for the past umpteen months, I was finally free. I got teary eyed as I lay there, staring up at the ceiling.

It felt like I'd lain there on my office floor for an hour, though it was probably more like ten minutes. I dialed Dave's number.

"Dave! What's going on, man? I hear you've got some news for me about these Fitness Revolution guys. . . . Well, *shyeah*—why wouldn't they be impressed?! . . . Oh, yeah? What kind of partnership opportunity? . . . That's true. I have been thinking about taking

on investors, but are they legit? . . . *Really?* Over two hundred locations? Hot damn! . . . They want to fly in when? . . . Sure, what the
hell? What harm can come from talking with them?"

I was sitting across a table from two guys silently staring into my eyes
as they waited for me to speak. Our table was tucked away in the back
corner of the dimly lit, dark wood restaurant. I took a long sip of my
IPA and weighed the pros and cons of the offer just pitched to me.

This would mean I would give up a big chunk of equity in the company.

*True, but the money they're offering and the access to their fitness net-
work would make Fit Food a national company overnight.*

But is it worth not controlling your own enterprise?

No, I'd still have majority percentage so I would maintain overall control.

*Nah, uh—not according to the golden rule: he who has the gold makes
the rules.*

"Specifically, how much are we talking here?"

Without blinking, the more talkative of the two, Aaron, said,
"We don't want to put a cap on it, so we'll start with what you asked
for, and we'll add to it as needed—whatever it takes."

Aaron was the entrepreneur and the face; he was the guy who did
the talking, made the connections, and whom everybody wanted to
be around and learn from. Jason, only a few years older than me, was
the corporate guy, the glue, the one who managed everything; he was
the one who enforced Aaron's decisions.

Aaron had a consistent personality. He had a confident, yet laid
back style of speaking, which always made him easy to talk to. Jason,
however, had two different personalities: There was his Mark Cuban
mode, where he was flamboyant, jokey, and easygoing. Jason had a
mansion in Kentucky, and when he was in Mark Cuban mode, he
would invite me over to play in his game room. He had basketball,
pong tables—ping and beer—and a virtual driving range simulator;
he even had bleachers so that when he hosted big events, people had
a place to sit and watch the action. But then there was his Numbers

Nazi mode, in which everything looked like a math equation to him, and he would rarely talk anything but straight business and *never* used facial expressions. When he was in Numbers Nazi mode, he sort of had a Ted Bundy thing going on: he was a young, handsome guy, but he would stare at you with his black, emotionless eyes for minutes on end while he calculated things in his head.

These guys were two of the biggest players in the fitness industry. They owned a fitness conglomerate under which they controlled two of the fastest-growing gym/personal training franchises in the world. They were looking for ways to increase their franchisees' revenues and generally control more elements of the fitness industry, and after having just finished a tour of my systemized kitchen operation, they saw me as a means to achieving this. Everything they offered sounded amazing: their infrastructure, their network, their funding for whatever the hell I might want or need. My hesitation was that these guys would be forming a board of directors, which meant it wouldn't be a one-man show anymore.

They were poker-facing me like pros.

"All right," I confirmed, "I'm in."

Their poker faces morphed into smiles and they shook my hand.

"Excellent," Jason said as Aaron picked up the check. "Why don't you fly down to Louisville next month for our annual conference so we can introduce you as our new partner? We'll have a suite reserved for you at the Marriot downtown."

"I'll be there!"

Jason and Aaron headed back to the airport, and I rushed home to tell Brie the big news.

PART 11

9

MEETING THE PUPPET MASTER IN LOUISVILLE, KENTUCKY

Over the previous few months, Brie and I had grown much closer. We couldn't stand to be away from each other, so we decided to move into a two-story suburban house together. Every house on our street looked pretty much the same; neighbors made small talk as they washed their cars; children bounced freely from freshly cut yard to freshly cut yard; we had a swimming pool, a tennis court, and there was even a neighborhood newsletter. I didn't feel at home there, but Brie was happy, and that was all that mattered to me.

Ever since the Saint Paddy's Day when Brie and I met, I had cut off all the other women in my life cold turkey—though I was unable to stop the onslaught of dirty texts from Sara. Every now and again, I'd be at dinner with Brie when my phone would buzz with a text, and I'd pull up my screen to find a nude selfie and something dirty written in Spanish.

A competition arose between us to see who could outsweet the other. She preprogrammed the coffee machine so that I'd have a fresh cup waiting for me when I woke up each morning, so I brought her breakfast in bed. Thoughtful handwritten love notes were countered by sporadic bouquets of flowers, nightly back massages were met with foot rubs, and ego-boosting compliments were matched by general admissions of admiration: "You're so smart. You're such an inspiration. I'm so proud of you. You're my favorite person." One evening, I said something to her that took this little competition to the next level, and I did it completely subconsciously, but I'll never forget her reaction to it.

"Oh, my god! Are you serious?" she asked as water started filling her big blue eyes. "I can't believe you just said that to me. You *love* me! I can't believe you said that you love me!" She started to smile. "Oh, my god." Her voice went up a couple of octaves. "I love you *too*!"

She pulled her cell phone from her pocket and started frantically pressing the screen, then she put it on speakerphone and held it up. "Mom, you won't believe it—Jeff just told me he loves me! It was so sweet! Here," she said as she stuck the phone in my face, "I'll let him tell you how he said it!" I wasn't sure of whether I was quite ready to start using the *L* word; I was still adjusting to the public handholding and the way she made a kissing noise every time she gave me a smooch. "*Muuuuah!*" But when I thought about it, I knew I did love her.

We even had a little family growing; it started with one sphynx cat Brie was obsessed with, then she wanted a second one for the first one to play with. When those two had kittens and she couldn't let two of them go, we were left with four hairless felines, which I swear Brie trained to walk under my feet; every trip downstairs became a death-defying test of courage.

We were now doing everything together, including flying to Louisville to attend my soon-to-be business partners' big event, Fitness Business Weekend—an annual event that Jason and Aaron hosted to which everyone who owns a fitness company was invited to come learn the latest fitness trends and how to use them to improve business. But our real reason for being there was to reel as many people as possible into Jason and Aaron's vast marketing web.

—

"Mr. Philips, we've been expecting you!" the concierge said with enthusiasm as he extended his hand to me. "We've got everything ready for you—including a bottle of Kentucky's finest small batch in your room—and your elevator key card for access to the twelfth floor, where your room is."

"Elevator key card? Won't the elevator take me to my floor anyway?"

The concierge did his best to hide his smirk. "Well, Mr. Philips, the twelfth floor is where all of our luxury suites and the cigar bar are located; they're only accessible to card holders. Here, this gentleman will assist you with your things."

As soon as the elevator door closed, my iPhone buzzed with a text from my soon-to-be business partner Jason. "Swing by the lounge, to your right when the door opens. We'll have a quick drink, then I'll walk you to your room. I wanna go over a few things."

I showed it to Brie. "He wants me to meet him at the bar for a quick drink. Want to go?"

"When was the last time you had a 'quick drink'?" she mocked me. "I'll be in the room getting ready for dinner."

When I walked in, he already had a glass full of some dark, delicious-looking liquid waiting on me.

Before I took my first sip, Jason dove right into business. "You know, we've got the mastermind meeting first thing in the morning, so we'll go over all the key instructions for the rest of the weekend there, but the most important thing you need to do over the next two days is befriend as many of these guys as you can. Do you have business cards?" he asked before chugging the rest of his drink.

"Nope," I said, then downed my bourbon.

He flashed two fingers to the barman across the room to signal another round as he continued, "Attaboy! Never hand out business cards at these things; these guys are all flustered small-business owners and they'll never get around to following through with you. You collect their cards, so the ball's always in your court." Our new drinks were placed in front of us as Jason continued, "I know you can talk a homeless guy into giving you his change cup, but don't stop there. Be aggressive: take these guys out for drinks tomorrow night after the conference, flirt with the women—and guys too when it applies—and, for God's sake, make everyone go drink-for-drink with you. You've got the gift—after five or six, you'll still be dead sober and they'll be cry-laughing at everything you say. You can't buy that kind of rapport."

In my room, over an entire liter of the smoothest bourbon I've ever tasted, Jason tried explaining to me and Brie what their business was and how the model worked, but because I was the first person ever welcomed into this fitness fraternity without having come up through the ranks, he'd never had to explain it before. Plus, the drinks had finally started taking effect on him, so the conversation ended with him slurring out, "Fuck it, we've got a ton of different moving parts, and you'll start to understand over the next two days."

Up until now, I had known these guys were savvy businessmen/investors, but I had no idea they had the kind of power I was about to witness.

At seven fifty-five a.m., when I walked into the conference room, Jason—in his frat-boy Mark Cuban mode—grabbed me and began the barrage of introductions: "This Mr. Clean–looking motherfucker right here . . ." We shook hands. ". . . He's the former editor of *Men's Health and Fitness* magazine. Jeff Scot Philips is our newest brand partner; he's the food dude. I have a feeling you guys will have a lot to talk about."

Jason tapped me on the arm and waved me in his direction as he walked toward an Italian-looking Irish guy who could have easily won a Ray-Liotta-in-*Goodfellas* look-alike contest. "Jeff, come this way for a second. I want you to meet our corporate strategist"—we shook hands—"he's a finance and real estate wizard. The only thing he does better than make everyone money is flap his jaw; in fact, we've got to walk away before he starts yappin', because this bastard was, unfortunately, born without an off switch."

In a deep Brooklyn accent, the guy replied, "*Fuuuuck yoooou,* Jase," as they both laughed. "Good to meet ya there, Jeff. Don't believe a word this jerk-off tells ya. Ya know, Jase, it's funny, just the other day I—"

"Hey!" Jason said as he placed his hand on Liotta's shoulder to interrupt him, "not to cut you off, but I want to introduce Jeff to a few others before we begin today. We'll be right back." He then guided me to a Poindexter-ish guy sitting alone staring at his laptop. "Dr.!" Jason shouted. The man's head popped up. "Jeff, I want you to meet our director of research and education material for the IYCA [International Youth Conditioning Association] and a professor at Texas Tech's Health Sciences Center. Doc, Jeff owns the bitchin' kitchen we've been telling you about."

Making our way through the room, Jason sped up the introductions. I met a TV personality from *The Biggest Loser*, a recognized face from *ESPN Magazine*, the creator of one of the world's largest online nutrition coaching companies, and tons of other fitness role models that I'd looked up to ever since I'd entered the health industry.

"Jesus," I asked in amazement, "is Dr. Oz himself here?"

Jason cracked a little smile. "Ha! No, but he is a great conduit." I wasn't quite sure what he'd meant by that, but I would find out soon enough.

Approaching the circle of people surrounding Aaron, Jason playfully wedged himself in between two of them to make room for us in the circle. "Guys, this is Jeff Scot Philips—the man with the meal plan. Jeff, this is Dave Schmitz—we just call him 'Bandman.' You ever worked out with exercise bands?"

I nodded and said, "Of course."

"They came from this guy. The lovely Jill, here, is our Infusionsoft expert; she builds all our digital marketing campaigns. She's the only person I know with a sailor's mouth foul enough to make every guy in this room blush."

Jill played coy. "Am I really that bad?"

Jason bumped me with his elbow. "Jeff, I once watched her have a screaming match with a big, 'roided, macho gym owner, and a few minutes of Jill insulting his manhood made him bow his head and walk away."

Jill turned to me. "Like they say, 'It takes a real cunt to make a big dick disappear.'"

"Oh, my *Gah-ha-hawd!*" Jason half chuckled as blood rushed to his face. "Thank you for not letting me down, Jill. Clint, here, is our master copywriter—he and Aaron do all the fitness education on the market. Clint will have you in a fetal position by the end of the day attempting a Turkish getup—he's obsessed with that shit." Clint gave Jason the middle finger as the rest of the circle laughed. "This is Dex. He does all of our social media traffic and conversions. He's a fucking genius—you two will be working together a lot. And, of course, you know Aaron." Aaron gave me a slap-five handshake, then pulled me in for a half hug. This gesture sent a message to everyone who saw it: Jeff is now one of us.

Ninety-five percent of the people in this room were members of the six-six club: they had six-pack abs and six-figure incomes—with the exception of Jason, Aaron, and a handful of others, who were comfortably in the sevens. The people I had just shaken hands with wrote the certification programs that your personal trainers and dietitian need to pass; they spearheaded the health curriculums taught at universities, crafted the messages spread by popular brands like *The Biggest Loser*, helped make P90X a household name, scripted the "education" that makes it into the trade journals that your doctor reads, filtered the health content that went to the fitness blogs and the top fitness magazines that you and your friends read, and served as the faces you see all over traditional media. Any health or fitness advice you see on TV, read about online, or hear from a health professional's mouth likely came from the people in this room.

These were the most influential names in the fitness industry, and despite the amalgam of alpha personalities, when Aaron spoke, every single person shut up and listened. Aaron was Papa Bear. Here was a guy I didn't know existed a month ago, and he was quarter-backing half of the entire health and fitness industry.

I had been in the game for years as a personal trainer, a nutrition-ist, a gym manager, and a small-time fitness guru, but as I was being brought up to speed on the ins and outs of Jason and Aaron's fitness conglomerate, I was learning that the health and fitness industry works just like commodities trading, with a handful of gatekeepers who control how the market runs, what sells, and what trends.

Together, Aaron and Jason owned a company called Fitness Consulting Group (FCG), which is an umbrella corporation that hosts dozens of other companies underneath it and trades thou-sands of other companies' products on what we jokingly—though not inaccurately—called the Fitness Stock Exchange (FSE). If you've ever done P90X, then you've invested in the Fitness Stock Exchange, and here's how.

Beachbody LLC is a multinational corporation, like FCG, run by Carl Daikeler. Carl isn't into fitness—though he happens to be the behind-the-scenes creator of *8 Minute Abs*—but is, rather, an infomercial guru who was looking for his next product to sell. He raised $500,000 from his group of investors and then approached trainer to the stars Tony Horton and asked him to create an ex-ercise plan that could be commoditized into a DVD set, which he did: P90X. Beachbody LLC then took the P90X product and sold it through its distribution channels—some of which it literally owned, like its fourteen million Beachbody coach affiliates, who use net-work marketing to sell P90X (on its website Beachbody unabashedly explains how you can use this multilevel marketing system to push out competitors' products), and some distribution channels it simply partnered with, like the Home Shopping Network, which is why you started seeing the product in magazines, in gyms, on blogs, and all over TV.

The Beachbodys and FCGs are the Goldman Sachses and the JP Morgans of the fitness world, picking and choosing every product you see and buy.

But here was the most jarring thing to me: now that I was sitting in on these decisive commodities meetings during which we discussed what would be sold through the FSE—such as my food or Dave Schmitz's exercise bands—I realized the conversations were a hundred percent about sales numbers, not what effects the products would have on consumers. They were just designed to produce the highest return.

Likewise, over at FCG, when we wanted to sell a certain program, diet, or specific food, it got pushed by the brokers out to the investors (gym owners, TV programs, fitness magazines, etc.), who then pushed it on to you. When you order your healthy recipe books or protein bars online, work out with an exercise band, pay membership to a gym, participate in a weight-loss challenge, buy a smoothie from a juice bar, or eat *my* food and supplements, that's all money in FCG's pocket. That's what Jason meant before when he said Dr. Oz was a conduit; Oz and others like him are used as distribution channels that help get consumers like you to buy into the commodities that companies like FCG create.

Now unless you're a gym owner or a fitness guru, you likely don't recognize Fitness Consulting Group or Beachbody by name—just like you've never heard of North Castle Partners, which owns Jenny Craig and Curves gyms, or Invus Group, which owns Weight Watchers International—but that doesn't mean they're not controlling every single thing you see and buy in the health industry market. These guys are in the finance game, which means they're a step or two removed from the consumer, while the ones directly "in charge" of the company—CEOs like myself—answer to them.

So here I sat in the middle of the six-six club, a room full of health and fitness influencers at what they unabashedly called their "mastermind meeting," as I watched the Puppet Master dictate what the upcoming trends were going to be and how they were going to enforce them.

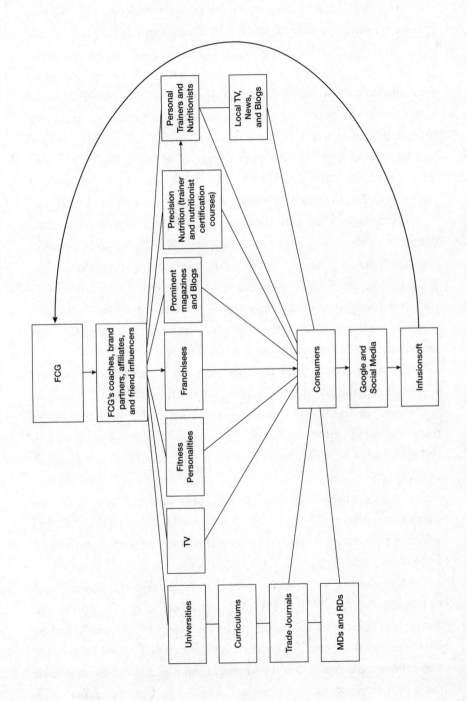

"OK, guys," Aaron addressed the crowd with the calm authority of a seasoned military commander, "here's the game plan for the next couple of months: group training has been a huge success—the per-hour revenue of personal trainers across the country has gone up fivefold by convincing clients to work out in groups—think boot camp or CrossFit—rather than one-on-one with their trainer. Next up, nutrition is going to be the new wave—food, food, and more food will be the hot topic for the next couple of months. We're going to start with done-for-you nutrition lessons designed by Clint, with all the current buzzwords like 'metabolism' and 'holistic,' and all that.

"Gym owners will buy these and then charge their clients, their clients' friends, and new prospects a small fee to come to a nutrition workshop. Keep in mind the big picture isn't the workshop revenue, guys, it's the upsells and conversion of new clients"—because FCG got paid monthly royalties from gym owners' revenue—"which is why our corporate strategist (Liotta) is going to teach the gym owners to hit their KPIs, to ensure they sign up more members."

Everybody jotted the bullet points as the Puppet Master continued pontificating the fitness industry's upcoming trends.

"Next, we'll crescendo to Precision Nutrition's thousand-dollar nutrition certification course for trainers. Nothing is being sold to the consumers here. The idea is to certify personal trainers as nutrition experts."

"A nice side effect of this," Jason chimed in, in a jokey tone, "is that their clients will be even more inclined to listen to their advice, which, of course, will be to buy our nutrition products and food." Everyone laughed.

"Once that promotion is over," Aaron continued, "we're going to be introducing Jeff Scot Philips's twenty-one-day detox program, along with the meals to match it." Everyone in the room turned to where Aaron was pointing, to see who the hell Jeff Scot Philips was. "And the good news is that it's rebrandable, which means you'll have the ability to put your own name and logo on it. The even *better* news is that Jill has the IFS funnels built and ready to be plugged into your software, so everything I just mentioned will be plug-and-play."

Whatever the hell IFS funnels were, the entire room seemed to be pretty excited about them. I would soon learn that IFS—short for Infusionsoft—was a software that all the industry leaders used to market products and services to consumers without them realizing it.

A guy in the back of the room raised his hand and Aaron called on him. "So, will the gym owners be able to sell this twenty-one-day program to their clients?"

"Yes," Aaron confirmed, "*but* this is ultimately an upsell promotion. Once customers buy into the program—or even if they don't—they get dropped into a drip campaign to purchase the gym's food. Jeff has sales scripts for gym owners and a done-for-you press release to get local news and radio into each gym for promotion."

"What about the trainers who promote a more gradual, holistic approach to weight loss?" the guy followed up.

Jason responded, "They can believe whatever philosophy they want; we're talking about sales here, and I want to see every single gym running some sort of twenty-one-day, twenty-eight-day, or six-week weight-loss challenge based on Jeff's material."

The guy put his hand down.

"Starting at the end of this month, the only thing coming out of every personal trainer's mouth should be *food*—speaking of which," Aaron said as he turned and pointed his finger at Mr. Clean, "Lou, can we squeeze a couple of nutrition articles in *Men's Fitness* to help this promotion?"

"You bet!"

I had just witnessed Aaron, the fitness industry's puppeteer, dictate the upcoming health trends and how we were all going to make a shitload of money in the process.

After another twenty minutes of reviewing the logistics of Aaron's master plan and assigning specific to-do lists to each person, Jason turned to one of his employees standing by the entrance to the room and shouted, "Sounds like it's getting pretty noisy out there, Bobby; let's do this!" And with that, the big doors swung open and the fittest sea of people I'd ever seen began flooding into the conference room. Every person had either a protein shake or a gallon jug of water in one hand; the other hand was reserved for handshakes.

Half of these people were the franchisees of my two new business partners, and the other half were about to be converted. Each year, health professionals—personal trainers, gym owners, physicians, chiropractors, nutritionists, and dietitians—go to health conferences like this one to get educated by experts in the industry. But Jason had instructed me the previous night that instead of educating them, the point of my speech today was threefold: (1) to stroke their egos and remind these professionals that they were the voice of the entire health industry, (2) to build rapport with them and let them know that I would help make their pockets fat, and (3) to convince them that my food products were the way of the future and they didn't want to miss out.

After an introduction from Aaron, I took the stage and gave the audience my sales pitch.

First, I set an epic tone: "There are more obese people in America than there have ever been, which means you have a very unique opportunity sitting in front of you—more so now than any other time in history—and that's the opportunity to save lives."

Then a cheesy one-liner: "I know you're all familiar with lifting heavy weights, but there's nothing heavier than responsibility; and every single one of you holds the weight of the health industry on your shoulders."

Next I buttered 'em up: "There are people out there desperately needing to lose weight. They need *your* wisdom; they need *your* expertise. You have a ton of power in your hands, because your clients will do anything you tell them to—you're their health professional— and that's a huge responsibility, guys.

Then I added a little moral obligation: "And I hope you don't brush it off as 'no big deal!' People are entrusting you with their livelihood, their medical bills, and their families' well-being, which is why it's more important than ever before that you help your clients make the smartest choices possible—for themselves as well as their children.

Then came the pitch: "Now, there's a lot of shitty food out there, and your clients eat it, unknowingly, every day. And this is why I've designed the ultimate meal solution, not only for them, but for you, as well."

Pointing to an audience member I asked, "You there, in the red shirt, where's your gym located?"

"Kansas City." The guy responded.

"Well, where's the Kansas City diagnostician going to send his hypoglycemic patients? To the Planet Fitness up the street so they can pay ten bucks a month—for life—to a gym they'll never set foot in? Or is he going to send them to the only health guru in Kansas City who can hand his clients a meal plan designed to cure type 2 *and* send them out the door with affordable, healthy food?"

Next, I made 'em an offer they couldn't refuse: "Look, your clients need these meals to change their lives. *You* need the meals to make your gym the number one gym in your city—and, let's face it, who here is going to complain about the extra three to five thousand a month from food sales?"

A brief pause for dramatic effect. And the sign-off: "If you want to be a part of something big, if you want to stand out from the overflooded sea of personal trainers out there, if you want to make a difference in this industry and actually change people's lives, then come see me after the conference, and we'll work together to make that happen!"

After the day's last keynote speaker wrapped up his presentation, the room erupted into hundreds of side conversations about dinner plans. I bounced from person to person, extending invitations. "Hey a bunch of us are going to the Hard Rock Cafe for dinner, and drinks are on me. We're all going to regroup in the lobby in an hour so we can share cabs. If you've got a business card, I can text you when I'm heading down."

When I stepped off the elevator an hour later, with Brie holding my arm, there was a group of fifty or so fitness pros waiting eagerly in the lobby. I walked into the center of the crowd, threw up my hands, and asked, "Who's ready for a drink?"

We got to the Hard Rock Cafe in the heart of downtown Louisville, and the manager snapped his fingers to pull every seat and table in the place together so they could accommodate our crew. Then the drinks started flowing like a NASCAR beer garden.

The woman to my left managed a gym in Illinois and was already tipsy—loud, red in the face, clinging onto my arm to make her points, and even drooling a little when she laughed. When I started making jokes about Planet Fitness, she started wheeze-laughing so uncontrollably, she plopped her head right into my lap. I quickly scooped her up and leaned her against the guy on the other side of her.

The following morning, when we regrouped in the conference center for day two of the event, it was as if I'd been friends with these health professionals for years. Starting the following week, they would all be selling Fit Food.

10

"UNLESS YOUR FOOD IS MAKING PEOPLE SICK, WE DON'T CARE. SINCERELY, THE FDA"

After I successfully passed Aaron and Jason's test with my performance in Louisville, the partners had their lawyers begin arranging all of our vertical merger documents. I was appointed CEO by the newly assembled board, which immediately started putting their fingers into everything. They inserted their bookkeeper into my company records, they shut down my S Corp and my LLC so we could form a handful of joint ones, and they shut down my business bank account and opened new accounts for our newly formed corporations.

We started having meetings upon meetings for *everything*. We would use Google Hangouts to dial in to a videoconference, since we were all spread out across the country. Very few things ever got decided in these meetings, but even when they did, it was never the result I wanted. One of our first "group decisions" was to change the name of the retail side of the company from Fit Food to a majority-voted Lean Eats, which I wasn't particularly fond of. Luckily, it didn't matter, since we were now primarily a production company, rather than a retailer, which meant the customers had no clue who was making the food they were eating anyway. We were now shipping CrossFit gyms packages full of "CrossFit Meals," Gold's Gyms were retailing "Gold's Meals," and customers who ordered our food online had no way of knowing they were on *our* website. They were ordering their food from what looked to be a food-for-buff-moms website, for example, so a few days after placing their orders, a cooler would arrive at their front doors containing meals labeled something like "Buff Mommy Meals."

The next group decision was for me to fire the majority of my old crew, so the partners could move the company headquarters to Elizabethtown and bring in their own staff to run all the operations. "It would be better to start fresh," Jason assured me. This little maneuver rendered everyone who'd helped me get my business off the ground jobless and put a few lifelong friendships on hiatus, which made me feel every bit the shitty friend I was for allowing it to happen. Stolichnaya served as an interim friend.

I was able to save Kevin, Babs, and, for some reason, Casey. They became my B-team chefs. Their job would be to design the new meals each month, which would be mass-produced by a new team of cooks in the giant production kitchen we were about to move into. Everyone else would be replaced by new hires. Jason and Aaron's giant team of fitness coaches replaced my sales crew, Vic, Roger, and—despite my attempt at taking a pay cut in order to keep him on—even Dave, who was the one who initiated the partnership with Jason and Aaron. At night, I laid in bed, wracked with guilt about letting him go.

I thought my life was going to fall apart without Emily around to juggle all the moving pieces, but despite my pleading, she got replaced by a manager named Logan, whom I referred to as Mr. Nervous-Food-Service because he was constantly paranoid that every little thing we did was going to get us into hot water with the health department. According to him, the equipment was never calibrated *enough*, the labels weren't ever accurate *enough*, the cooking procedures weren't thoroughly detailed *enough*.

Previously managed by my well-trained team of six, all customer service calls were now handled by one person, Suzy the robotic script reader, which meant that if she was on the other line, then you were listening to hold music. And when a customer finally did get to speak with her, she wouldn't even adjust her dialogue to match the gender of the person on the other end of the phone. "I do apologize for the inconvenience, ma'am or sir," she'd say in a frustratingly cheery tone, "I'll look into this right away." Then she would breeze right along, as if she'd actually solved the issue. "Ma'am or sir, are there any other issues I can assist you with in the meantime?"

Nobody ever said it out loud, but it was evident that her job was to frustrate callers to the point of giving up. She would routinely tell customers she was going to transfer them to the specialist in such and such department, who could better assist them—of course, no such person existed—and then she would put them on hold for ten minutes before hanging up on them. The ones who had the energy to call back then had to sit through another ten minutes of hold music interspersed with the occasional, "Thank you for holding. Your call is very important to us. Please remain on the line."

After we had remodeled the staff, Jason the Numbers Nazi wanted to pump a bunch of money into marketing.

A computer algorithm is making you fat. This algorithm is called a digital marketing campaign—dozens of which you're likely locked into at this very moment, and one of which is possibly mine—built inside a program called Infusionsoft (IFS), which connected to the back end of our brand-new thirty-thousand-dollar website.

This website was a thing of beauty. Not only was it designed to strategically guide visitors through a sales process, but on the back end, it tracked customer purchasing habits so we could better tailor future sales pitches via discounts and special promotions. It also used algorithms to produce spreadsheets that managed our entire inventory, along with a P&L breakdown that tracked all of our affiliates' sales. It alerted FedEx of our package count and shot all the necessary information and shipping labels to the kitchen each morning. The most impressive thing it did, however, was create an automated customer engagement system run by the IFS software.

IFS observes, tracks, and adjusts to everything you do, from the links you click or hover your mouse over to the emails you open or delete, the YouTube banner ads that you think you're ignoring when you close them, the things you search for on Google, the Instagram posts you like, the number of times you open a Web page, and practically anything you do on Twitter. Based on your behavior, you get filtered into one of these virtual algorithms—one you'll probably never even realize you're trapped in—that tailors our advertisements to match your needs, wants, patterns, and personality traits.

And to answer your question, yes, we can see you. We can tell where you are when you see our marketing—at home, at work, on vacation in Europe—how long you looked at it, whether you clicked through or not, and, of course, whether you bought something. It sounds a little NSA-ish but don't worry; because there are so many people we're trying to target, we don't ever take the time to follow an individual. We're typically just looking at numbers on a spreadsheet trying to spot overall trends based on your behavior.

How does this work?

A very commonplace tactic we use to move products is called a drip campaign. Let's say we want to increase our paleo meals sales because they've got a decent margin. We'll design a campaign algorithm like the one on the previous page to start following you around. Maybe the software noticed that you watch *The Biggest Loser* and you tend to "like" its social media posts, so it responds in a couple of ways: First, it starts posting banner ads on *The Biggest Loser*'s page and whenever you watch one of its videos on YouTube. Next, you'll start seeing links to headlines and getting emails educating you on the health benefits of a paleo diet, all the while programming you to (a) believe that this is scientifically backed nutrition information, and, more important, (b) recognize the word *paleo*.

Then the software gets *really* sneaky.

Because it knows exactly where you're located, it will start using emails along with a software called SlyBroadcast that leaves prerecorded voice mails that sound like they're highly personalized—not to you, but to the fitness experts in your area. These calls offer to help increase the fitness expert's business profits by encouraging them to promote the paleo diet to people like you in their local community.

The software then sends these fitness experts press releases—written by used car salesman Clint—that they can use to send you emails and physical ads, submit newspaper articles, and spread the message through television segments in your area, all discussing the health benefits of the paleo diet. You start seeing how popular the paleo diet is everywhere you look, and you start to think, *Hmm, maybe I should see what all the fuss is about*, and what a coincidence that the little coffee shop you visit, the co-op you frequent, the gym you work out at, the banner ads on YouTube, your Facebook feed, and the bottom of the *New York Times* article you just read, *all* happen to have paleo-friendly meals for sale.

Gotcha!

"Not me," you might be thinking. "When those annoying ads pop up on my screen I just X them out. I don't fall for this kind of stuff!" But what I'm telling you is, *you* don't have to pay attention to our marketing for us to get to you. I was able to witness, from the inside, just how stealthily this type of marketing can affect you.

Remember how I told you we don't ever take the time to follow an individual? Well . . . I did it once—just as a test—and here's what I saw.

A good friend of mine, a practicing MD, was notorious for taking whatever new nutrition info she would read or hear about, and then turn around and spread it to her patients. One such patient happened to be a client of mine too—the infamous Libby. During this time we were in the middle of searching for an industrial kitchen so we could ramp up our food production, and so over the next couple of transitional months, we wanted to drive consumers to buy supplements like smoothies and protein bars—which we were also now labeling privately and selling to retailers—instead of our food. To achieve this we designed an IFS marketing campaign to educate health experts, like Libby's doctor, on the benefits of counting calories—that sugar was calorically equivalent to protein, and that real food was equivalent to supplements, and therefore you could interchange them as long as you kept track of your calories. Over the next couple of months Libby's doctor got bombarded by the IFS drip campaign— on her social media, her email accounts, the blogs she read, and even on her local TV news—and just like clockwork, my MD buddy had relayed the message to Libby.

I was checking in with Manny—who was now training Libby— over the two-month life of the IFS campaign, and he showed me that she had been gaining a steady three pounds per week. When I asked Libby whether she'd been doing anything different, she told me that, per her doctor's recommendation, she had been replacing her meat-and-veggie meals with Reese's smoothies and protein bars because they had fewer calories. As a result, after two months of following this nutrition philosophy, she was now twenty-three pounds heavier. She hadn't even directly seen any of our Infusionsoft marketing. The campaign had made its way to Libby through a credible influencer— her doctor.

The goal wasn't to make people gain weight; the goal was simply to sell more of our product, and this type of marketing software was insanely effective at achieving this.

We use the most seemingly minuscule consumer actions, demographics, and psychographics to adjust our information and products on the market. Consumers' heights, ages, the shows they watch, and the things they search for on Google will determine how we get them to buy our products. Even the number of children people have allows us to manipulate them.

For example, did you know that people with kids eat at least ten more servings of sweets per month than people who don't have kids? So, in order to get parents, who are trying to eat less sugar, to eat *more* of it, all we have to do is advertise to their kids. Children watch twenty-eight hours of television per week, twenty-one hours of YouTube, and who the hell knows how many hours of those epileptic Vine videos, so by engaging them there, we can convert them into our little sales soldiers. As a result of your kids lobbying you for our sugary foods, we'll work our product's foot in the door, which gives the parents a 76 percent chance of eating it.

Once we'd gotten our marketing system in place, my next task was to find an industrial kitchen to move into.

I headed back to Virginia and started searching for a new kitchen space. Between being on the road so much and moving into a new neighborhood, I hadn't seen the Extortion Cougar in a couple of months. She simply didn't know where to find me.

I'd gotten word from Manny that a woman fitting the description of the Cougar had been frequenting Fit Studio, asking for me. My first day back in my gym, I was in the middle of doing a seated shoulder press with two heavy dumbbells above my head, sitting right beside one of the gym's very first members, sixty-five-year-young Linda, when the Cougs walked up, right between my legs, stuck her hands down the front of my pants and death-gripped me. I froze. Linda looked down at the Cougar's buried hand, then looked up to make eye contact with me.

The Cougar said nothing; she just stood there, cupping me while she waited for my arms to give out, which they quickly did, and I had to drop the weights onto the floor by my sides.

I got a membership at Gold's Gym the next morning.

I don't know who squealed, but it didn't take the Cougar long to learn I was there. At first, she tried waiting for me at my car, but when I saw the trap, I shared my conundrum with a fellow gym member and gave him a twenty to pull my car right up to the front door. After a handful of failed parking lot assault attempts, the Cougs started coming into the gym, right in front of everyone, and chasing me around. Nobody intervened. I suppose it was pretty hilarious to watch me weave through the rows of exercise machines, fleeing from an attractive woman.

I got a third membership, this time at ... *sigh* ... Planet Fitness. I knew nobody would think to look for me there, and I started rotating randomly among the three gyms. I also started going to the gym at sporadic times throughout the day to ensure my safety.

After a few weeks of searching, I found an industrial kitchen to move our main operation into. It was a forty-three-thousand-square-foot warehouse with long rows of shiny ovens, loading docks, freezer trucks for food transportation, and even USDA-regulated temperature-controlled rooms. The cooking room remained at seventy-two degrees, the main prep room stayed at thirty-five degrees, and the storage room was kept at negative-ten degrees Fahrenheit. If you had a cup of water in your hand and put your arm through the door to the room, the water would begin to crystallize in seconds.

The staff had a field day with the storage room.

The guys loved to hide outside the freezer room door and wait for Li'l Mikey—one of the newly hired cooks, who was only an inch or two over five feet—to walk in without a heavy jacket on, thinking he was just popping in for a quick second to grab something off the shelves, and then slam the door shut and hold it closed. After a couple of minutes, Mikey would start banging on the door and pleading for his freedom. "Fuck you guys—this joke isn't funny! I can't feel my fingers; open the door, you assholes!" he would yell, as the guys stood outside the door giggling like schoolgirls.

Poor Li'l Mikey didn't do well with cold stuff in general.

Dry ice is one-hundred-and-nine degrees *below* zero. One day we ran out of dry ice, which got delivered once a week, and Mikey drew the short straw to go pick up extra. Unfortunately, none of the guys knew—or, as I suspect, chose—to tell Li'l Mikey that dry ice eats oxygen, which is why it's normally transported in tightly sealed five-hundred-pound drums, but when you're transporting a lot of it in open air you've got to drive with the windows down. The reason it's such a dangerous task is that when dry ice eats the oxygen in a confined space, it doesn't produce a suffocating sensation; it produces a euphoric, sleepy sensation that makes you want to comfortably lean your head back and rest your eyes. Thank the lawsuit gods that Mikey made it to the loading docks and put his car in park before he went unconscious behind the wheel. Luckily, one of the cooks was taking a load of trash out back and spotted Mikey fast asleep with his car running, and reported it to the rest of the crew, who ran outside to save him.

Mikey wasn't allowed to handle dry ice again after that.

In our new kitchen we were assigned a liaison from the US Department of Agriculture, whom I came to know as USDA Eddy. He made sure that everyone on the floor wore hairnets and outer jackets to neutralize the inevitability of someone wearing a shirt to work that was covered in cat hair. And unlike in my previous operation, we were then required to have a formalized sanitization process, along with specific kill procedures for when we had to dispose of waste. And we also had to have what's called a HACCP (hazard analysis critical control points) system, which is a fancy way of calling a very detailed-and-documented process for handling every single piece of food: the temperature it gets cooked to, the temperature it gets chilled to, the temperature it gets packed at, how long it sits on the cooling rack, at what time it is vacuum-sealed and by whom, and so on.

USDA Eddy explained to us that we had to document every single step of the process for every single action surrounding every piece of food that passed through our kitchen. If someone had to cover his mouth to sneeze, and then had to run to the nearest sink to wash his hands, it was documented. If a tray of chicken breasts was overcooked and had to be disposed of, it was documented. If the guys locked Li'l Mikey in the freezer room for five minutes one morning and another five that afternoon, it was documented.

You might think that documenting every minute detail of daily operations would help keep food companies honest, but you'd be sorely mistaken. This actually allows, if not outright encourages, food manufacturers to bend the rules, because the USDA didn't actually monitor our real-time operations. Instead, every single thing we did was monitored in retrospect. The only way the USDA knew that we cooked each chicken breast to one hundred sixty-five degrees to ensure against salmonella was that we said that we did it in our activity log. The only way the USDA knew employees were washing their hands after leaving the bathroom was that we documented it in the activity log. The only way the USDA knew that the food that ended up in our customers' mouths was compliant with all the health and safety guidelines was by checking our activity log. *For Chrissake!* This was more of an invitation for fuckery than when my third-grade teacher let my best friend Adam and me swap papers and grade each other's quizzes.

Having USDA Eddy on-site also meant that we were now required to use "accurate" food labels to list our meals' ingredients; however, this process was highly informal and riddled with all sorts of loopholes, many of which USDA Eddy taught me.

Eddy was on my right, sorting through our food labels, and Brie—who had recently quit her sales job to become my full-time business partner—was on my left, taking notes with a pen and pad, as we walked through the kitchen.

"What's this 'paleo' word here mean?" Eddy asked when reviewing my packaging for approval.

"Oh, that. It's just a trending buzzword at the moment. It supposedly means this is the type of food people ate during the Paleolithic era."

"Hmm, well, I can't approve that."

"Oh," I said deflated. "I guess we can take it off the label, but that's going to hurt our sales with the CrossFit gyms."

"Well, hang on there, Mr. Philips; you don't have to go taking it off the label. Let me show ya a little trick: if you slap the word 'friendly' after the word 'paleo,' that'll make it OK."

He was teaching me that compound words were somehow above the law, like when he rejected our buffalo chicken meal because it wasn't from Buffalo, New York (seriously, that was his reason), but allowed us to call it "buffalo-*style* chicken." I wasn't sure whether there were actual rules about this stuff or ol' Eddy just had strange lexicon pet peeves that he liked to enforce.

"OK." I sifted through the labels, leaning on Brie's pad to scribble "friendly" on each one, then handed them back to Eddy. "Here you go."

"Hold it there." He handed the majority of them back to me. "I only need to see the chicken and beef labels."

"What about all these others: pizzas, breakfasts, desserts, seafood, veggies?"

"Nope. That stuff's out of my jurisdiction."

"Who inspects those, then?"

"Well, everything other than beef and chicken technically falls under FDA jurisdiction, but nobody's going to inspect those while I'm here, so they're good to go."

"So, you're saying I *can* call the carb-free pizza 'paleo' without adding the word 'friendly?'"

"You can claim your peanut butter brownie contains no peanuts, for all I care. I just cover the birds and cows, brother."

"You're messin' with me . . . "

"No, sir. Do what you please with the rest of the labels."

"Oh, so, then you'll only need to check our nutrition facts math for the beef and chicken meals too, right?"

"Me? Do math?" He laughed. "That'll be the day! Just get your dietitian to put some numbers together, I'll give 'em a once-over, and then you'll be good to go."

"You don't oversee the process?"

"Nah. As long as you use a registered dietitian, that's good enough for me. We mainly care about the ingredients list."

Brie and I returned to the kitchen a few days later with the nutrition facts from our dietitian—who, by the way, was an RD (registered dietician)—though Eddy never inquired about her credentials.

"Mm-hmm, mm-hmm." He sorted through the labels. "This one's good. This one's fine. *Hold it!* There's no way these serving sizes are accurate." He passed me a label for our meal.

"Really? Hmm. OK, well, I can get her to recheck the math on them if need be."

"Now, before you go wasting all that time reworking what's on the labels, why don't you just change your company's category to weight loss on your business license. It'll be a onetime fix, so we don't have to have this conversation again."

"I don't understand. What does that do?"

"See, if you list yourself as a weight-loss company like Weight Watchers, instead of a food company like Heinz, you aren't required to list accurate portion sizes on your meals. You can make a portion whatever the hell size you want."

"Are you serious? How is that even allowed?" I asked Eddy. Brie had slightly scrunched lips and was shaking her head in disbelief.

"Oh, it's another political loophole; some Republican probably got paid off by one of your competitors."

I couldn't believe my ears! As a nutritionist, I'd spent years teaching people how to decipher food labels and the importance of the nutrition facts numbers, portion sizes, number of servings, etc., and this government agent standing in front of me—the guy who was supposed to be keeping me in check—was telling me he didn't give a shit? Not only that, but he was teaching me—hell, *encouraging* me—to lie on my labels.

Practically, the only thing Eddy couldn't advise me on was the marketing claims I was allowed to make when advertising our meals. I figured taking out a full-page ad saying, "Our food cures cancer!" would be pushing our luck—though I'd found a plethora of research suggesting that it might be true—but was I at least allowed to say, "Our food helps reverse type 2 diabetes?" USDA Eddy had no clue, nor did his boss, nor *his* boss's boss. Nobody from the Department of Agriculture could give me a straight answer regarding what I could legally say about my food. "If you're that concerned about your marketing claims," Eddy eventually suggested, "I would just get the FDA on the phone and ask them."

"Food and Drug Administration." The woman's voice sounded annoyed. "This is so-and-so. How can I help you?"

"Hello, yes, I'm trying to find out what sort of claims my company can make about our healthy meals."

"That's really not what we do here. You'll want to call the FTC to get approval on any product claims."

"OK, do you have a number I can—Hello?"

"Federal Trade Commission." This woman sounded equally annoyed. "This is so-and-so speaking. How may I direct your call?"

"Yes, I was told to call you guys to find out what claims I'm able to make about my health-food products. For example, can we claim that they're helpful in reversing type 2 diabetes?"

"I'm sorry, sir, you'll need to contact the CPSC to find that out."

"You're joking. I was just told to call you—that the FTC handles food product claims."

"Yes, sir, but you're asking about consumer product safety claims, not actual food claims."

"OK, but I—"

Click.

"Thank you for calling the Consumer Product Safety Commission. So-and-so speaking. How can I help you?"

"Yeah, I'm just trying to find out what health claims I can advertise about my company's products. I just got off the phone with the FTC and they told me to call you guys to find the answer I'm looking for."

"I'd be happy to assist you. What kind of claims are you trying to make about your products, sir?"

"I want to know, for example, whether I can label my meals gluten-free."

"Oh, it's a food product?"

"Yes."

"Then you'll need to speak with the FDA, sir."

"Yeah, but I already—"

"Would you like me to transfer you?"

"Oh! Sure, that would be great! Thank you."

"One moment."

"Hello?"

"*He-llooo?*"

Click.

God damn it!

"Food and Drug Administration." I recognized the irritable voice. "This is so-and-so. How can I help you?"

"Look, we spoke just a few minutes ago. I'm trying to find out what kinds of health claims I can make about my food products. You sent me to the FTC, they sent me to the CPSC, and *they* directed me back to you guys. Can you please help me out, please?! I just want to make sure we're up to code and not breaking any laws or anything."

"I can help you, sir, no problem."

"Oh, thank God!"

"Has your kitchen been inspected?"

"Uh, yeah, what do you need to know?"

"What's your facility's FDA code number?"

"Oh, no, we're actually a USDA-inspected kitchen."

"I see. Well, I'm sorry sir, but in that case, you'll have to check with your United States Department of Agriculture representative to find out what claims you're able to make about your products."

"I already checked with them and they said they don't handle that; the FDA does."

"We do, sir, but only for FDA-inspected kitchens."

"Well, do you want to send someone out to inspect my kitchen?"

"Sir, if you're already working with the USDA, then you're outside of our jurisdiction."

"But *you* don't know that I'm under USDA jurisdiction. We're just talking on the phone here."

"Well, are you?"

"Yes."

"OK, then, sir. The only way the FDA will have any interest in visiting your USDA facility is if consumers start contacting us to complain that your meals are making them sick."

"Are you—are you serious?"

"That's correct, sir. Is there anything else I can help you with today?"

"No, but we haven't solved anyth—"

"Thank you, have a nice day."

Click.

I wasn't mad that they weren't helping me, or even that they kept hanging up on me. I was mad at the forethought of us making claims about our food, and then, years later, some asshole from one of these very agencies I'd just called stepping in and busting me for breaking some law that they wouldn't even tell me existed. I needed a drink.

It was just after lunch and I was already sick of drinking wine that day. I had fifteen minutes before that day's conference call—just enough time to zip around the corner and pick up a bottle of Stoli from the ABC store. Red Bull would make up for the caffeine I was used to getting from the coffee. *I won't go overboard.* I laid the ground rule. *Just enough to calm my nerves, so I can get through this call.*

"Fuck it," I told everyone on the videoconference, "I can't get a straight answer from anyone about health claims, so let's move on." Brie was sitting just off camera beside me, half listening as she rapidly typed away at whatever she was working on, on her laptop.

"OK," Jason spoke up, "the next thing on my list is ingredients."

"What about the ingredients? We've got them down to a point."

"When I went through the list, I saw a lot of unnecessary

amenities we can cut back on—for example, almond meal is about three times the price of starch, and that special oatmeal you use for the tuna cakes can easily be replaced by regular oatmeal, if not bread crumbs."

"Yeah, but we use those things for the gluten-free line."

"Nonsense," Jason said matter-of-factly, "we'll swap them out. Also, all these various herbs and spices that we use for seasoning are superfluous—salt can be used uniformly, which would save a ton. And I noticed we're using Stevia as a sweetener in the dessert items. Sucralose is much cheaper."

"Isn't sucralose bad for you?" Jill chimed in.

"I don't know that it's any worse than Stevia," I said, "but, yeah, sucralose is certainly much more stigmatized in the media, and so if people see it on the label, they'll freak. Same for the gluten stuff."

"Well," Jason said, "there's your answer: just don't list it on the label."

Brie's thunderous typing came to a dead halt. There was an awkwardly long pause. After a minute, the white noise in the background seemed to have gotten so loud, it was hurting my ears.

I broke the silence. "You mean, like . . . use it, but . . . omit it?"

"You said it yourself," Jason confirmed. "You don't know that it's any worse than the other sweetener, so what does it matter which one is listed on the label?"

I looked over at Brie, who was shaking her head at me while sternly mouthing the word "no."

"I—I don't know, man . . . " I hesitantly said to Jason.

"OK, everybody," Jason said, "let's go ahead and wrap up this call. We'll go through the rest of the list on tomorrow's call."

With that, everyone said good-bye and hung up. Then my phone rang. It was Jason.

I answered, "What's up, man?"

"Listen, Philips, when we make decisions on these calls, we need you to own them. It looks bad when you sound uncertain—like you're not on board with us. We need to know you're a team player."

I mixed another vodka bomb before Brie grabbed the bottle from me. "But we hadn't made a decision yet," I said. "We were in the middle of talking it out."

"You're the food and nutrition guy, right? When you make a decision about that stuff, I back you on it. My job is running the numbers, so when I say we need to make a change for the sake of the P&L sheet, I need you to support me."

"Fair enough, but you're encroaching on my territory—you're talking about changing the ingredients."

"Philips," he said in a stern tone I'd never heard before, "this is just a simple, insignificant change to the ingredients, but it'll make a huge difference to the bottom line." Then he quickly changed back to a lighthearted tone. "We're partners now. Don't you want *our* company to do well?"

"Of course I want *our* company to do well." I rolled my eyes for Brie to see.

"OK, then. Why don't you go ahead and email everyone at the kitchen and tell them to make the switch, buddy? And copy Aaron and everyone in on it, so they know you're on board with the team."

"Maybe you should be the one to tell everyone; it's your decision, Jason."

"You're the boss, Philips. Orders need to come down from you." He then, once again, switched to a faux-bro tone. "Take charge, brother. Own that shit!"

"All right," I said.

Brie stood up and turned to leave. I tried grabbing her arm, but she pulled away and shut the office door behind her.

"I can do that for the seafood and stuff," I continued on with Jason, "but USDA Eddy's going to shoot down the chicken and beef labels in a heartbeat."

"You're a resourceful guy; I trust you'll find a way to make it happen."

That irked me. Yet, even though I knew he was making an unethical decision that would have a negative impact on our customers, I emailed the group and told them about the changes.

After a couple of weeks of trying to sneak various versions of the nutrition labels by ol' USDA Eddy, Jason called to check on my progress.

"How are those labels coming along?" he asked. "They done yet?"

"No, he keeps rejecting them. The new, cheaper ingredients are listed in the operations manual for the chefs to go by, so he knows they're supposed to be on the nutrition label."

"Philips," he said as he switched to the stern tone, "we need to find a solution quick, OK, buddy?"

"I don't know what we can do. I can't take it out of the manual—the chefs work like robots and they'll fuck up the recipes without them listed in there."

"Well, I trust you'll make it happen."

For the previous few years, I'd been giving money to the Miss Virginia organization, partially as a favor, and partially because having these young attractive women promoting my meals was a great advertisement. So I called the current Miss Virginia, who had just returned from competing at the Miss America pageant and, because she hadn't won, had a little time to spare for a friend. I dropped her off at the kitchen for a few hours, wearing a short black skirt, where she was to spend the afternoon with USDA Eddy, making flirty small talk, asking personal questions, and tugging on his arm as she said she was dying to try the new meals as soon as he approved them.

When I checked in with Eddy the following morning, our inaccurate labels had miraculously been approved. This earned me an "attaboy" from Jason.

So, big deal, I told myself, *our customers think they're eating Stevia, but it's actually Splenda; one processing plant's ingredient versus another*. I was able to convince myself after my second Yellow Tail of the morning. But gluten was different.

"We can't just omit it from the label," I assured Jason. "People can get sick from that shit, you know?"

"Can I trust you'll find a solution to that?"

"Jason!" I said, annoyed. "There's no solution to find. We have to stop advertising that we've got gluten-free food."

"Philips, that's not an option."

"Well, then *you* need to find a solution!"

"I don't want to get into an argument with you, buddy. Why don't you just do some research and see what you can come up with."

After a few vodka bombs and a handful of phone calls, I'd found a solution.

I'd still been talking with Papa John's executive chef sporadically, so I'd been keeping a close eye on its business. When Papa John's announced its new gluten-free pies, I convinced my celiac friend and her husband to try one. When she told the Papa John's employee on the phone that she'd been diagnosed with celiac disease, he recommended against her eating its gluten-free pizza because it "couldn't guarantee against cross contamination."

I checked out Pizza Hut to see whether it was any better and it was just as blatant. Right on its website it said that the sauce—made by Hershey's—used on its gluten-free pizza could contain gluten. So the pizza companies were shouting "We've got gluten-free pizza!" to reel customers in, but when someone with an actual gluten allergy asked whether it was safe to eat it, the pizza places would tell them, "We recommend against it."

I borrowed their strategy and built a safety net into our customer service scripts to prevent true celiacs from ordering, which incidentally produced a funny little case study on hypochondriacs. Any time someone tried to place an order and asked whether the food was gluten-free—and they frequently did—customer service was trained to respond by saying, "Yes it is, *but* we can't guarantee against cross-contamination, so I don't recommend you order any food." And can you guess what response this evoked? Out of the tens of thousands of customer inquiries we documented as claiming a gluten allergy, every single person—with the exception of one or two—said, "You know what? I'm sure I'll be fine. I'd like to place an order anyway." This made me feel a little better about our misleading labels, because it confirmed what I'd assumed since 2009, that 99.9 percent of people who *thought* they had a gluten sensitivity either didn't have one or it didn't bother them enough to stop ordering the food.

I wasn't proud of what I'd done, but I justified it by thinking to myself, *this is the last shady thing and from here on I'll play it straight*, which, of course, wasn't true. Nothing we did was ever enough to quench Jason's thirst for revenue. Every other week, it was *some*thing—cutting a minuscule cost here, tacking on a hidden fee there. One trick Jason enforced was the "one dollar" technique: Every so often, we added just one dollar to a price—bumping from $147.99 to $148.99, for example. The customer wouldn't even notice, but multiply that one dollar by, say, twenty thousand people, and that's an additional twenty grand.

It was all about the bottom line.

11

THE COUGAR ATTACKS

After a year of being partners with Aaron and Jason, I would have thought we might have established a monthly revenue that Jason would be happy with. I was wrong.

"Last month's numbers weren't as high as I'd projected," Jason said. "We need a boost."

Sensing where this conversation was going, Brie beat my hand to the vodka bottle on my desk and disappeared into the other room with it.

I put the phone back to my ear. "We could promote another weight-loss challenge."

"No," he shot me down. "That's too short-term. Your chefs at the second kitchen enjoy putting their culinary skills to work, though, right?"

"Yeah, I guess."

"Well, I just emailed you a list I put together—some new meals that they'll enjoy making. We'll send them out to our best customers as a sort of focus group, and they'll respond and let us know which food they like and want to order more of. Take it to the B-kitchen this morning and have the chefs get to work on it."

I pulled up the email and skimmed through the list of meals. "I've got to say, Jason, this list doesn't look like it'll fall inside our nutrition guidelines."

"Maybe not, but that's OK. This is just a test—we're not changing anything yet."

"Yeah, but if customers try these new meals and decide they want them moving forward, we'll have to make them. And I can tell you, just from looking at these, that my whole weight-loss program will unravel with these recipes."

"Let me handle this, Philips. You don't worry about it."

"I don't know, man—"

"For fuck's sake!" Jason raised his voice. "What is it with you questioning every single thing I say?"

"I'm trying to make sure we're making the smartest decisions here, and you're fucking it up right now!" I snapped back.

"It's a focus group, Philips! The whole point is you ask consumers what they want so you can better cater to their needs. Don't you want to give our customers what they want?"

"Yes, we've been over this, but if—"

"OK, then," he interrupted me in a calmer tone. "Now that that's settled, I'll expect to have the new samples ready by the end of the week."

There was no point in continuing to argue with him; besides, I needed to save my energy for the battle with Cryin' Kevin that I knew was about to take place.

I walked into the other room to find Brie power-cleaning the kitchen in silence.

"What's the matter?"

She spun around. "You're changing!" she blasted.

"How am I changing?"

"The Jeff I know wouldn't do this kind of stuff to his food, to his labels, or to his customers."

"Babe, it's just a minuscule change. Come on, the customers are still—"

"And you think *this* is helping you?!" She held up the vodka bottle. "This is numbing you! It's making it easier for you to go along with this crap!"

I knew she was right, but all I could do was stand there silently.

"We're supposed to be partners," she continued, "but I don't want to be part of a company that does this sort of thing." Then her face softened. "And I *certainly* don't want to watch my prince drink his decent, human intuitions away."

"You're right," I spoke up. "I know you're right. I'm just *really* stressed and I—"

"I know you're stressed, baby," she said as she set the bottle down and wrapped her arms around me, "but you're better than this, and I want you to promise me you're not going to be like those Nutrisystem assholes you hate."

"I promise."

Her giant blue eyes teared up as she nodded in agreement, then she pulled me in to kiss her.

I printed the new recipes to take over to the test kitchen.

When I turned the key in the ignition, my gaslight came on, which I paid little attention to. But as I drove to the kitchen in the morning traffic, I thought I remembered having filled the tank the night before. I knew I had a good twenty miles after the light came on, anyway, and the kitchen was only five miles away.

About halfway to the kitchen, the car erupted into a violent convulsion; the frame was rattling like an earthquake and the steering wheel was vibrating in my hands. I looked down at the dashboard to see that the needle was *way* below the E. *Damn it!* The entire car was shaking as it attempted to suck the remaining drops of gas from the bottom of the tank, and there was nothing I could do in the middle of that busy road but cross my fingers.

I was rolling along at fifty-five miles per hour when I felt the power steering go out, all the dashboard lights come on, and the engine go dead. When the car slowed down to a manageable speed,

I hopped out and began pushing it. I needed to keep the momentum so I could get it into the big parking lot up ahead on the right. I glanced up at the sky and saw my own neon face staring down at me. *How humiliating!* There I was, in the middle of the road, pushing my dead vehicle right underneath an electronic billboard with a huge close-up picture of my smiling fucking face on it. People were honking their horns as they passed, and I could feel my phone buzzing in my pocket, undoubtedly from people texting to razz me.

After about twenty yards of huffing and puffing, I got the car into the lot and looked underneath to see whether there were any signs of leakage—nothing. I pulled out my phone, called Brie, and asked her to come scoop me up.

As I waited on the side of the road, my legs dangling out the driver's side of my lifeless SUV, I skimmed through my texts. There was a barrage of jabs from people driving by; the producer from the daytime talk show I frequented had turned my dilemma into a comical headline. "On today's show, local fitness expert JSP shows us how you can squeeze a workout in during your commute to work." My chiropractor friend asked, "How many miles to the gallon does your rickshaw get?" One of my old clients chimed in, "I like your new training regiment, but put some *oomph* into it!" Even the president of the Roanoke Chamber of Commerce got in on the fun. "Hey, Fred Flintstone, they also make cars with fuel injectors, now. #yabadabadoo."

I would respond to them with a smartass rebuttal later; right now I needed to text Chef Kevin to make sure he was on the schedule for that day. "The fuck do you care?" he replied back. "I should be asking whether *you're* scheduled to work today—when was the last time you did any work, ACOMF?" ACOMF translated to air-conditioned office motherfucker, a title he had endearingly assigned to me. "Well, [crying emoji] Kevin," I playfully typed back, "it's getting a little chilly in my office, so I thought I'd come visit you guys in the—" I was jolted so violently that I dropped my phone into the road as I felt a hand go right through the bottom of my shorts and grab my scrotum. The Extortion Cougar was standing between my legs, and I knew it wasn't by coincidence.

I grabbed her forearm. "*You* emptied my tank, didn't you?" I asked, though I already knew the answer. "Do you know how fucking crazy that is?"

"You think you can just avoid me?" she shot back. "Do I have to remind you that *this* is mine?" She pulsed her claws, sending a vomit-y shockwave up into my stomach.

It was both frustrating and arousing to think that this woman had so much power over me. I wanted to fight back and win. Or did I want to fight back just so I could lose?

I stuck my hand down the front of my pants and attempted to wedge between the little fingers clenching the life out of my nuts and pry them off. She applied more pressure as she threatened me. "Take your hand off," she said and assured me, "or it's only going to get worse."

I started worrying about the long-term effects that this abuse might have on me. I let go of her arm.

Then I heard a woman's voice calling my name from behind me, and I turned my head to look. Brie was parked on the other side of my car.

"Hey, babe!" I shouted to her. "This is a friend of mine from the gym. She saw me parked over here and stopped to chat." The Cougar looked over my shoulder and released a hand to wave with, and then started kneeling down into a squatting position. I sat frozen for a minute, feeling completely helpless, as she continued fondling me right there in front of my unknowing girlfriend. When I heard Brie open her car door the Cougar released a hand, reached down, and picked up my phone off the pavement, then stood back up and waved it to Brie.

"He should really protect his valuables better," said the Cougs as she gave me another painful pulse with the other hand.

Brie confirmed, "Yeah, I'm always telling him he needs to get insurance on that thing."

Then the Cougar whispered to me, "This was your last get-out-of-jail-free card," and then, waving good-bye to Brie, she left.

I had about ten minutes before the B-crew would be walking through the door to start the day, and I was already exhausted by all the changes being made by Jason and the tank-pumping, relationship-jeopardizing encounter I'd just had with the Cougar; I needed to calm my nerves.

As quickly as I could, I downed two Big Gulps—a full bottle and a half from our dry red inventory—and I then had a *teeny* buzz setting in, just enough to take me back to ground level. Just to be safe, when I heard the sound of Kevin's minivan backfiring as the morning crew pulled into the parking lot, I bypassed the coffee and bottoms-upped the remaining half of the second bottle. The chefs and cooks all came shuffling through the door, bringing with them the smell of their morning cigarettes.

"Hey, Kevin! The sun is shining, the birds are chirping, and how are you doing on this fine morning?"

He tried to hide the hint of a smile on his face as he replied with his standard "Fuck off."

Everyone laughed.

"Oh, come on, now, my jovially challenged buddy; what's the matter?" I extended my arms out to my sides with a giant, cartoonish smirk on my face. "Do you need a good-morning hug?"

"Fuck away from me."

"Let me tell you something, Kevin, you're good enough, you're smart enough, and, doggone it, people like you!"

"Jesus Christ," he said as he rolled his eyes. "Did you dump your load into one of your cheap whores before you came in this morning or something?"

"No, I let your mother sleep in, but I do have great news for you: you get to design a new menu today!"

"What the fuck?!" he laid into me. "Fucking pricks in your ivory tower coming down to bark orders while l work my ass off."

"Work your ass off?" I raised my eyebrows.

A mixture of laughter and affirmations came from the crew. "*Bwah ha-ha!* He's got ya there!"

"Whatever. Do you want me to put on a little hat and dance for you too? I'm not your fucking puppet," he said, still hosting a hint of a smile. "So fuck off with your new fucking menu."

"Kevin," I said as I pointed to his face, "you've got a little cheer right there. You might want to wipe that off," which exacerbated his smile. He turned away to hide it.

"Fuck you."

I laid the piece of paper on the table in front of him. "Here are the specs for the new menu, and there's something here you'll actually enjoy. This food can be as butter-drenched, salt-smothered, and fat-fraught as your nonexistent heart desires." I punctuated my remark with a smack on the back. "Have fun!"

Over a few *fucking assholes* and a couple of mumbled *piece-of-shit-thinks-he-can-tell-me-what-to-dos*, Kevin began working his magic.

By the end of the week, the "health-food" samples Kevin put together could not have been picked out from a fast-food lineup. And, whether I liked it or not, the paying customers that we were about to ship these meals to would be determining our menu and ingredients from then on, which meant the food I was loading into my car was important, *really* important.

Mold forms at thirty-eight degrees. This was a fun fact that I had to keep in mind as I transported food across town from the test kitchen to our USDA kitchen, where we would ship it out to the focus group. If the temperature of this food had gotten above thirty-seven degrees, the meals would have been compromised. After I crammed the last bag of food into my car, Chef Kevin handed me a thermometer to put into one of the bags.

As soon as I pulled out of the parking lot, my gas light came on. The Extortion Cougar had drained my fucking tank again. I still had a gallon or two left in my backup tank—which I *would* have used to get to a gas station if I hadn't been pressed to get the food into the freezer before it got above thirty-seven degrees, so I hoped I could get across town on a few drops.

I couldn't use the air conditioner without risking sucking up too much juice. Without it, I would have had maybe twenty minutes, give or take, to get the food into the USDA freezer. It was about a fifteen-minute drive to the production kitchen. *I should make it, as long as I don't have to stop for gas*, I thought to myself.

I was sweating bullets. At each stoplight, I would start from second gear instead of first, and once my RPMs got high enough, I would skip third and shift straight into fourth to save gas. On hills, I would put the car in neutral and let it roll as far as it could.

After fifteen of the sweatiest minutes of my life, I pulled into the kitchen's giant lot and swung around to the back of the building to the loading docks, the nearest entrance to the freezer room. As my luck would have it that day, USDA Eddy was standing right inside the door, and as soon as I stepped into the kitchen, he stopped me in my tracks when he saw the giant bags of food I was carrying.

"Whoooaaa! Whatcha got there, Mr. P?"

"It's a long story, but I've got to store this food here for the night. This is Jason's law," I assured him. "It's shipping out with tomorrow's orders."

"Jeff, off-site food is outta my jurisdiction," he said as he waved his hand. "You know I don't give a shit about that." Then he looked to his left, then his right, and whispered, "But you know you can't bring it in here—especially not from an FDA kitchen!"

"Come on, be a pal," I pleaded. "You gotta help me out here. This is our focus group food, you understand? It has to get shipped out tomorrow morning, no matter what." Eddy held his palms up. "Jeff, please! That's impossible; if those bags stay here overnight, I'll be a jobless man tomorrow."

Out of the corner of my eye I could see Logan's two little eyes peering over the top of his computer monitor through his floor-to-ceiling window that overlooked the entire production room.

"It's food, not rat poison, Eddy."

"I understand, but you're asking me to risk my fucking job. As long as it's prepared in here, you can ship anything you want—put dog shit in the package, for all I care, just no outside food."

I took the opportunity to keep the conversation light. "Dog shit? We're not Nutrisystem, Eddy!" which made him chuckle. "But, listen," I pressed him, "Jason's gonna chop our balls off if this food doesn't make it to the customers."

Without taking my eyes off of Eddy, I swatted my finger in Logan's direction and he quickly ducked his head back behind his computer monitor. "You've got to meet me halfway. Do me this favor, Eddy."

"What can I do?" he said as he raised his hands to his shoulders. "If my sup does an inventory check and finds food being stored in the freezer that isn't accounted for in the activity log, it's my ass. He comes in tomorrow to find a ton of extra meals on the books and an empty freezer, it's your ass!"

I reached into the bag and checked the thermometer: thirty-four degrees. Time to play the trump card. "Come on, Eddy, do it for Miss Virginia. She's dying to try these new meals."

He let out a conflicted sigh. "OK, look, no doubt my supervisor's going to check tonight's inventory, so there's no way this food can be in here prior to that. But if it's stored somewhere else overnight, I come in at nine a.m.," He winked. "Know what I mean? The only way I know what goes on between inventory count and when I get here is by reading the activity log. If I didn't see it and it's not documented in the log, it didn't happen." A Cheshire cat smile swept over my face. "Whom do you want me to bring in here next, Miss North Carolina? Miss Pennsylvania? Miss America?!"

The mere thought of all these young, attractive women made him revert into a bashful choirboy. "Shoot, I don't think I'd even be able to speak to them!" he muttered with his eyes fixed on his shoes.

"How about another visit from Miss Virginia, then?"

"Aw, hell, I don't want to trouble her; I'm sure she's got better uses for her time . . . but, I tell ya, a signed picture from her would keep me busy for a while—she's a little heartbreaker, that thing!"

I threw my arm over his shoulders. "Come on, at least give me a challenge, Eddy. I'll have that on your desk when you come in tomorrow," I said as I winked at him, for emphasis, "at nine a.m."

I would scramble over to my vacant condo on Longview, where I'd store the food for the night and then take it into the kitchen first thing the next day. My morning crew began packing the food containers at seven, so I would meet them there with the samples and have the shipping packages sealed by nine, when Eddy would get in; we would just omit that detail from the activity log. On the way, I texted Miss Virginia and told her I needed a signed headshot for Eddy.

As I pulled onto my street, I reached behind me into the bag and pulled out the thermometer to glance at the temp: still thirty-four. *Phew! Plenty of time to spare.*

I crept up Longview to make sure the Extortion Cougar wasn't camped out, waiting for me—the coast looked clear, but I didn't see any parking spots in front of the building, so I drove right onto the sidewalk, grabbed as many of the bags as I could, and sprinted to the front door. While I was fumbling to find the right key I dropped one of the bags and the food containers spilled out onto the floor. *Are you serious?!* I found the key, opened the door, scooped up the containers, and used my cell phone light to rush through my dark apartment toward the kitchen. When I opened the fridge, a wave of heat smacked me in the face. *God damn it!* I started skimming through my phone, desperately trying to think of friends nearby who would let me use their fridges for a couple of hours. Then I remembered, *what about the two giant retail fridges in the back of Fit Studio?!* I scooped the bags back up and tossed them back into my car, praying I had enough gas to make it to the gym.

While I was sitting at the red light at the end of the street, the car went into another empty-tank convulsion. The gym was about half a mile to the left, but a football field distance to my right was a gas station. I reached behind me into the bag and checked the thermometer: thirty-*five* degrees. Choosing the gas station would put the food at risk, but if I didn't get gas, I might not even make it to the gym at all.

I jerked the wheel, turning a sharp right from the left-hand lane, and glided in neutral as far as I could into the gas station. I jumped out, hit regular unleaded, and swiped my card: declined. *Son of a bitch*! I forgot Jason had shut down the old business accounts to form yet another LLC, and the new AmEx hadn't arrived yet—and, as my luck would have it, Brie had my debit card to book a flight, car, and room for a trip we were taking to LA. Flustered, I stuck my hands underneath the driver seat and started scraping around. *A nickel . . . another nickel . . . a dime . . . yes—a quarter!*

After a minute of car-floor groping, I scraped together a buck-ninety-eight and ran in to pay the cashier. While I was feeding my poor, thirsty car, I reached back and checked the thermometer: thirty-*six* degrees, *shit*! I yanked the nozzle out, shorting myself a couple of cents worth of gas and flew down the road toward the gym, ignoring red lights. I pulled into the parking lot, swiped my key card, and started sprinting toward the back of the gym with half a dozen bags of food on each arm.

I turned the back corner and ran straight into the Cougar in the middle of a workout. I nearly knocked her over. I was defenseless, my arms each lined with giant bags of food, and without hesitation, she bypassed my denim armor and shoved her hand right down the front of my pants. "Why have you been hiding this from me?" she said as she squeezed.

"Listen," I said trying to reason with her, "I'll come right back here and talk with you, but I've got to get this food into a fridge *now*!"

"You're not going anywhere."

The food was going to spoil and Jason going to murder me, and for once in my life, I was trying to make a relationship work; I didn't want to be with anyone other than Brie.

Annoyed by my hesitation, she increased the pressure, "*Christ— OK!*" I lowered my arms and let the bags slide down and onto the floor. "Well, what do you want me to do?" I asked, as if I hadn't known the routine by then: First, she would spend a couple of minutes trying to break my jaw on her pelvis, then she would pin me down and turn me into a human trampoline.

Without easing up on her grip, she ordered me to take her pants off. "Pull 'em down."

"Right here?" I asked. "What if someone walks in?"

"Pull 'em *down!*" she repeated.

As ordered, I reached down and pulled her tiny pink workout shorts—no underwear—down below her hips, letting them fall to her ankles right there in the back corner of the empty gym.

I was panicked at the thought of the food being ruined and the investors' wrath that would follow, but there was a scalding-hot, bottomless woman dominating me—which she had by now successfully turned into a weird fetish of mine.

She was trying to pull me toward her, but I was pressing against the front of her thighs—stalling the inevitable in hopes of some sort of divine intervention. But then she grabbed a second fistful of hair.

Then a surge of muscular force rushed through my arms as I shoved her, sending her flying backward, until her bare ass slammed against the padded gym floor. Unfazed by the fall, she immediately started to get back up, but thankfully, her shorts were still around her ankles, hindering her progress. I scurried up the food bags and dashed toward the back.

"Bring that thing back here!" she screamed as I jammed the food into the fridges, at thirty-seven degrees *exactly*, and then bolted out the back door.

12

CHEESE AND SUGAR ON EVERYTHING (EXCEPT THE FOOD LABEL)

The week after my latest Extortion Cougar run-in, I was standing in the test kitchen, refilling my 13-percent-by-volume Starbucks, when my phone lit up. It was Jason. I took a few deep sips from my cup and answered.

"Yeah," I said without bothering to mask my apathy.

"Starting next week, cheese goes on everything."

I pulled the phone away from my head and looked at the screen in disbelief. "Cheese on everything? Why the hell would we do that?"

"They'll buy more," he said as if this should've been obvious to me. "What else is there to talk about?"

As predicted, our focus group had confirmed what Jason already knew and what I had feared.

We had two different customer demographics to accommodate. The first category was the taste chasers; these were the people who just wanted palate-pleasing munchies, whether they were actually healthy or not. Because these customers paid such little attention to what they put into their mouths, they were both the easiest to please and the least-consistent purchasers, so we had to continually excite them with new recipes and weight-loss promotions.

Then there were the label fables, the people who made all their dietary decisions by reading ingredient lists and nutrition facts. They were a trickier group to please. For example, they initially refused to eat our French herb chicken dish because the label told them that the light sprinkling of mixed-herb seasoning had xanthan gum in it. So we sent them our newer chicken Parmesan dish, with all the minute ingredients from the label omitted—a legal loophole called "discrete ingredients"—but more on this later. Instead of listing xanthan gum, maltodextrin, corn syrup, corn starch, the sugar in the tomato sauce, or the preservatives in the melted cheese, we only listed the very basics: sauce, cheese, chicken. And with no knowledge about what was *actually* in their food, these label fables choked it down, praised the taste, and demanded more.

But *all* customers demanded good taste, which meant loads of salt and fat. This led Jason to his conclusion: "Starting next week cheese goes on everything."

That day he was apparently in Numbers Nazi mode—calculating, irritable, and unwilling to waste energy on excess dialogue. "If two plus two equals four," he loved to say whenever I brought up things like ethics or customer recidivism, "why would we waste time talking about two's feelings or four's opinion?"

"These people don't need more cheese," I tried to remind him. "They're trying to lose weight."

"It's sales 101," Jason said as he snapped right into a business lecture. "You don't sell people what they need; you sell them what they want. If consumers want fat and salt; we're going to give that to them."

"Well that's shortsighted," I fought back. "Eventually, if people aren't getting good results from our food, they're not going to keep buying."

"Look, we don't need predictions here; we need sales," he

corrected me. "We're not worried about five years from now. We're worried about next month's numbers."

"Well, why don't we offer them two different options for each meal, so they at least have a choice."

"Phi-*lips*," he said tightly, "let's not do this fucking dance. We're going to change the goddamn ingredients and give them what they want. Now, I already spoke with Logan—he's expecting a call from you to discuss the updated HACCP." Jason knew the best way to get me to do something with production was prime the new kitchen staff for a change behind my back. "I made it clear to Logan that his livelihood is riding on the sales performance of this new food line, which means you better get them pushed through the USDA today."

Great, I'm the bad guy ruining our food; I'm the one lying to our customers; and now I'm the asshole boss threatening our employees' job security too. I'd had enough of Jason fucking up *my* company.

"Listen, Jason: we're not going to be a company that does this type of shit to our customers. They trust us right now, but if we—"

"*Jesus Christ, Jeff!*" he shouted over me. "I'm not having this discussion with you. We've got a warehouse full of employees whose jobs depend on this, along with thousands of small-biz affiliates who are losing hundreds of thousands right now, and they all depend on our sales to feed their families!" I could hear him slam his fist against his desk. "You want to be a good guy? Go home, and take Brie some fucking flowers. You want to run a business, buddy? You put on your big boy pants and sell shit!"

"Jason, you need to lib up, pal." Jason and I always discussed things in terms of liberal versus conservative, so this was political lingo for *you need to be nice.* "Of course I'm in business to make money, but you actually need to *give a shit*"—FCG's company credo—"about the people we're selling to. We're a weight-loss program, *buddy*, and nobody's ever going to lose weight eating food with a bunch of cheese and shit all over it."

"*Listen, motherfucker!* We're not here to review each customer's medical chart—fucking little shit! Yes, on paper, we're a weight-loss program, fine. In real life, we sell food. End of discussion, goddamn faggot motherfucker!" I couldn't help but crack a smile at his little tantrum. "Now, if we don't get the changes made and get this machine running, and I mean yesterday—cock-sucking piece of shit!—we're not spending another fucking dime. We'll pull everything. Got it?" My smile disappeared. "Stop thinking with your vagina and turn on your fucking brain!"

I was afraid of being left penniless, company-less, and stuck with the knowledge that the customers would continue to buy shitty food somewhere else.

"Fine," I said as I shook my head in defeat, "I'll take care of it, goddamn it." I took a deep swig of my Merlot latte. "I'll go talk with USDA Eddy now. When he gives me the thumbs-up"—I sighed—"I'll get Logan started on the new HACCPs."

So, once again, I made the fearful midday trek between kitchens. I hated this drive—my BAC was now constantly at a misdemeanor level, and I was also fearful of an attack from the Cougar. I took a back route to the kitchen.

"Hmm, mm-hmm," USDA Eddy mumbled as he skimmed over the piece of paper in his hand. "Sorry, Mr. P, I can't approve these new recipes."

"What are you talking about?" I fired back. "Why not?"

"You're a weight-loss company that sells lean, healthy meals, and with the fat being this high—all this cheese and crap—your meals will get bumped out of the healthy category. Oh, and that reminds me, the steak and salmon have too much fat in them to fall into the healthy category, so you're gonna need to take them off the menu."

"Are you fucking kidding me? We've been selling those for months and you never had a problem with them before."

"You didn't use to list the nutrition facts on your seafood, since you didn't have to, but with these new labels you've got, my sup told me these two dishes gotta go. You can switch to a leaner cut of beef, but the salmon is a no-go for sure."

"What?!" I shouted. "Salmon's, like, one of the healthiest things a person can eat!"

"Maybe so. I dunno." He tossed his hands up.

"And you don't even regulate seafood, so why the fuck does it matter?"

"It's got nothing to do with the salmon, Mr. P; it's the nutrition label. When you didn't have one, there was nothing for me to check, but by listing the nutrition facts, I can't just ignore it."

"That's absurd, Eddy. I list nothing and you guys couldn't care less; I accurately list what's in the food, and you say no?"

"Look, if you're that determined to sell salmon, why not just do away with the nutrition facts?"

"Because customers want to know how many calories and grams they're eating! For fuck's sake, what are the numbers we would have to meet to make it healthy and lean, and all that?"

"There are no set numbers—"

"*What*?" I interrupted. "How can I possibly meet guidelines the USDA doesn't have?"

"Hang on. Let me finish. There are no set numbers *because* the guideline is about the ratio of fat grams to total grams in a serving, and these numbers you have listed here don't meet that ratio."

"That's the dumbest thing I've ever heard. That's got nothing to do with health!" I smacked the paper out of his hand. "We're not changing everything because of that stupid code, Eddy."

"Don't do this to me, Jeff," he pleaded. "Don't put me in this spot. I'm not the bad guy here."

"Well, you're not exactly being helpful." I took a giant sip of my Big Gulp. "You act like we're the only company selling this stuff. Lean Cuisine sells salmon and beef, so how do they get away with it?"

Eddy looked down to his shoes and pleaded, "Jeff, why don't you just change the menu, please?"

"That's not an option, Eddy. There's no chance in hell Jason's going to bend on this one. Why don't you want to tell me how to solve the problem?"

Eddy mumbled back, "Because you're not gonna like what I tell ya."

"When was the last time I liked anything you told me. Just lay it on me."

"Well it's . . . I mean . . . I just don't—"

"Goddamn it, man! Out with it!"

Out of the corner of my eye I saw two little eyeballs pop up over Logan's computer monitor.

"OK, OK, but don't say I didn't warn you." Eddy leaned in close to me. "Have you ever seen a Lean Cuisine meal without some kind of pasta or bread in it?"

I shrugged my shoulders, irritated. "I don't know."

"What you've gotta do is put another type of food in with the salmon that doesn't have fat—something like pasta or bread, or anything sweet, really—so that the total grams of food in the container go up while the fat grams stay the same; this evens out the ratio."

"What the fuck, Eddy?!" Logan's head disappeared behind his monitor like a Whack-a-Mole. "You're telling me I have to put sugar in my food?"

Eddy started fanning his hands at me. "I know, I know. I told ya you weren't gonna like it."

"So you're telling me that if a meal has too much fat, we don't decrease the fat, we just increase the carbs so the fat doesn't seem as high?" I squinted my eyes and leaned right into his face. "You're going to stand here and tell me that the US health code says a bowl of sugar cubes is legally healthier than a plate of plain salmon?" I shoved his chest to make sure I had his attention. "*Do you understand how stupid that is?!*"

"It's stupid, I know, but I don't write this stuff, Jeff. Come on, I just have to enforce it."

"Get your sup on the phone." I pulled my phone out of my pocket and shoved it in his face. "This is insanity."

"No, please," he said as he put his hand over the phone. "That won't do any good. He's got no authority on that. If you yell at him, you're just going to get me in trouble."

"This is the most irresponsible law I've ever heard of! My mother eats this food, Eddy!"

"I'm sorry Jeff—I really am—but that's code. And please don't try to 'Miss Virginia' me on this one. There's really nothing I can do to help you this time."

Great, so now our "health food" was going to be covered in salt, cheese, *and* sugar. *Christ!*

My phone buzzed in my hand. It was a wordless text from Sara: five eggplant emojis. Delete. I chugged my Big Gulp, then dragged the back of my hand across my mouth to rub the purple wine stain off my lips.

"Fine, Eddy." I waved my hand at him. "Add whatever you have to on the labels and push 'em through. I just need this done today."

It seemed like every month our revenue wasn't as high as the projections, and therefore, we had to keep tweaking something—our ingredients, what we said on our labels, the marketing claims we made about them—in order to boost our bottom line. To achieve this, we were taking advantage of every legal loophole that existed.

I mentioned using "discrete ingredients" on our food labels earlier. Well, here's how this works:

The Discrete Ingredients Tactic

By packaging two or more different foods together, intended to be eaten at the same time, food companies get to use what are called "discrete ingredients" on our labels. This means that, instead of listing what each food item is made up of, we can just list the food itself *as* the ingredients. For example, we might sell a protein peanut butter brownie and a low-carb pan-fried pizza. When sold separately, we have to list everything in them: starch, maltodextrin, salt, sulfide, etc. But by coupling the brownie with the pizza as one "meal," we can just list the ingredients in "discrete" terms: pizza contains cheese, tomato sauce, oregano; brownie contains peanut butter, whey protein.

The Portion Size Tactic

If I market myself as a weight-loss company instead of a health-food company, like Weight Watchers does, I don't have to follow the guidelines for portion sizes. I can literally make my portion sizes whatever I want.

After making this irresponsible semantic switch, I created a few different portion sizes—no longer based on any nutritional guidelines—for customers to choose from. Typical customers got the regular-size meals, and customers who exercised with a trainer more than three times per week (helping my PT affiliates sell more training) were recommended to purchase our "athlete" portions. This forced more people to buy the meals. For example, when a husband and wife do a weight-loss challenge together, if the man has bigger portions and the woman has the smaller ones, then each of them has to order his and her own completely different set of meals.

The Polarizing Tactic

I'd learned this sneaky little strategy from a fellow health-food entrepreneur. My old friend, Jeff the Stoner Kitchen Owner, owned a small prepackaged, carryout food business for which he created full family dinners each week. He would put all the ingredients and cooking instructions in a giant bag with the frozen, uncooked food, and then all the customers had to do was throw everything into the oven and, *voilà*, dinner for four was ready. Jeff had also discovered an interesting tactic to drive up more food sales. When you walked into Jeff's kitchen, there were two side-by-side freezer sections: one with "regular" food for people who purchased based on taste and low prices, and one with healthier options, like organic and gluten-free food. What Jeff had actually done was take one meal and put two different labels on it: one was "healthy," listing nothing but the actual raw ingredients, and the other label had purposefully added "scary" ingredients like high fructose corn syrup, gluten, corn starch, etc., and then the price was marked up on the "healthy" label. It seemed counterintuitive to add bad ingredients to a food label that didn't actually contain them, but to my complete surprise, he actually moved *more* product this way and at a higher price too.

His health-conscious customers would unquestioningly pay more for the exact same food that, ironically, the more aloof eater would pay less for. This was because, as Jeff explained, affluence was directly tied to food consciousness; i.e., people who made more money, and therefore had the means and the desire to spend more on food, want to believe that they're getting the higher-quality product for that extra money.

Some of my meals were then listed as gluten-free and some weren't, but in reality none of them were actually gluten-free anymore—the label was the only difference. But consumers who had been taken by the gluten fad were happily paying twice as much for the same food that other consumers bought at the regular price.

The "Dwindling Serving Size" Tactic

As I already said, I can determine my own serving size portions. However, what you probably don't know is that I am allowed to base my nutrition facts on a single serving size. And I can also choose how big that serving size should be. When you take both facts into consideration, the nutrition facts label becomes pointless, because I can bring the numbers down to as low as I need them be as. The numbers on our nutrition facts label—the grams and calories—were like the T-1000 from the *Terminator* movies; I could bend and morph the serving size and servings per container as much as I needed in order to manipulate the calories and grams into a number that suited whatever narrative consumers wanted to hear. If one of our meals contained twenty grams of sugar, we simply chopped the serving size down to four per container, and listed five grams of sugar on the nutrition facts label. And because consumers never paid attention to serving size anyway, they were unaware that they were eating an extra fifteen grams of sugar.

Even worse than that are the trans fats.

Legally, as long as the trans fat per serving is equal to or less than 0.5 grams, we were allowed to list them as zero on the label. People are afraid of the words "trans fats." So to keep the customers happy, we just needed to make sure that our food labels *said* zero trans fats. All we had to do to achieve this was chop our serving sizes down and then up the number of servings per container until the grams of trans fats fell into the desired range. Nobody could stop us from marking a food that actually had five grams of trans fats at zero grams, simply by listing the servings per container as ten.

Consumers didn't notice it, and the FDA and USDA didn't care about it.

The Distribution Tactic

Consumers were mostly conscious of the fact that ingredients are listed in order of quantity. To combat this, we distributed sugars, for example, among varying types, so that sugar doesn't appear near the top of the ingredients list. For example, we combined sucrose, sucralose, high fructose corn syrup, brown sugar, dextrose, and maltodextrin to sweeten a food, so that there wouldn't be large enough quantities of a given *type* of sugar to hold the top position on the ingredient list. And since half the sugars I just mentioned were fake sugars, only half of them would be reflected in the nutrition facts numbers.

This fooled consumers into thinking there was hardly any sugar in the food they were about to consume, while in reality there was very little that *wasn't* pure sugar.

The Label Padding Tactic

This one was pretty straightforward, and you've probably heard of it before. Basically, what we did was pad the ingredient list with minuscule amounts of great-sounding ingredients—the kind of buzzwords that people recognize as being healthy—to give the food the illusion of health. Cereal companies are the kings of this; they throw in the faintest sprinkle of fiber, omega 3s, natural vitamins, and minerals just so they can claim it on the front of the package, which triggers your brain to think, *Hey! I recognize these words! This product must be good for me.*

The "Masking Scary Words" Tactic

Whenever an ingredient becomes publically stigmatized, instead of eliminating it from our food, we just call it by one of its other names. Consumers are afraid of the letters MSG, for example, so, instead, we're legally allowed to use alternate names for it—soy protein, whey protein, calcium glutamate, yeast extract, things you're not afraid of. Instead of saying sugar or high fructose corn syrup, we can list fruit juice, honey, or agave nectar.

The second ingredient listed in a food is important because label readers know there's a large amount of it, and since the words "sulfite" or "preservatives" would sound really bad, we use a better-sounding term, like "currants," which—although derived from a fruit—are still a processing-plant preservative.

The Fat-Free, Sugar-Free, Gluten-Free Tactic

We often use these claims on things that never had fat, sugar, or gluten to begin with, because we know it attracts eyeballs. Cereals say they're low fat all the time, but they were never high fat. The phrase "no sugar added" is another full-blown hoodwink that I'm allowed to take advantage of. It means that no sugar or artificial sweetener was added *during* the processing and packaging of the food, but that does not mean there aren't tons of pure sugar in the product already.

And don't forget, as you learned from my USDA salmon fiasco, that terms like "low fat" and "low sugar" are relative terms, meaning that if the grams of fat are low *compared* to the grams of sugar, then the food is low fat. If we want to claim low fat on a highly fatty food, all we have to do is up the sugar.

The Distraction Tactic

Some of the less relevant—though just as fiery—stigmatized terms in the consumer consciousness are "free range," "cage-free," and "humanely raised." Again, here are some labeling loopholes: Free range, in regard to cows and pigs, isn't a designation regulated by the USDA, so that claim on a label is fanciful at best. We use cage-free as a feel-good, purchase-boosting buzzword, but in no way does it mean that the purveyors we buy from are supplying us with humanely treated chickens. Speaking of which, the phrase "humanely raised" has zero regulation, so the humanely raised chicken you ate for dinner last night could easily have been the recent loser of an underground cock-fighting ring, and the USDA doesn't give a single shit.

The "Ingredients Claims" Tactic

As you now know, the FDA does not regulate any claims regarding ingredients, which means a couple of things. Blueberries, for example, are trending as a healthy food at the moment. Some loose science out there suggests blueberries are good for your heart. So just by adding a few to our cinnamon porridge, we're free to claim things like "Blueberries reduce risk of heart attack," naturally implying that eating our meals will reduce your risk of heart attack. Was this true? Heart attacks come from an accumulation of a lot of unhealthy habits, so it's unlikely that eating blueberry porridge would make much of a difference either way. But being able to make such claims about our food certainly increased our revenue.

The Copacking Tactic (Also Known as Private Labeling)

The FTC had a weird rule restricting us from claiming things like "You'll lose seven pounds in seven days on our food"—even when it was true—but given that we were producing food for retailers and branding it under their name, rather than our own (think Wal-Mart's

Great Value brand, which is actually produced by various third-party manufacturers), we were able to bypass this rule. Since our retailers weren't the ones producing the food, the FTC didn't have jurisdiction over them, and therefore we simply handed our marketing material to the retailers and let them make our health claims for us.

The "Cleaning Up the Ingredients" Tactic

This takes the cake as possibly the sneakiest and most detrimental tactic of them all. This was another lesson I learned from Jeff the Stoner Kitchen Owner. He would follow the health-food activists—the Food Babe, Mark Bittman, Michael Pollan—and take note of whatever new horrible ingredient they were preaching against (red dye, for example). Then he would tell his customers that he was "cleaning up the ingredients," and his food was free of red dye. At no point did his meals have red dye in them, but by following the popular activists' trendy buzzwords, the label conscious flocked to purchase the new "zero red dye" meals he was advertising.

Why is that so bad? you might wonder.

You might have read about the Food Babe's campaign to get BHT (butylated hydroxytoluene) out of cereals a little while back, and, sure enough, General Mills agreed to do it. She also got Chick-fil-A to remove food dyes and corn syrup from its batter, and Subway to remove some other unpronounceable ingredient from its bread dough.

The reason this is bad for consumers is that *even* if General Mills, Chick-fil-A, and Subway removed all of these potentially harmful ingredients, the poor Food Babe followers—thinking that their beloved comfort foods would be safe to eat again—would return to eating sugary, fatty meatball subs, fried chicken, and cereal! The food industry wins; American consumers lose. Could anything possibly contribute more to obesity than this?

Do you think activists like the Food Babe annoy us food companies? Hell no. She, incidentally, turns us into heroes when we leap at the opportunity to remove X ingredient from our food, making it "safe to eat again." She's free advertising for us!

You've seen the industry do this a million times. When food activists told their followers that sugar was bad, we switched to Splenda; when Splenda was bad, we switched to Stevia—and some back to sugar. But consumers kept eating the same junk food all along. Activists demanded fewer calories, so we amplified our foods' taste with sugar, instead of fat, which is far less calorie dense. And in some cases, we cornered both sides of the market by having our affiliates send media outlets "new research" suggesting that calorie counting was a waste of time, and that consumers should focus on avoiding sugar, instead. This way, our sugary *and* fatty meals would sell, all because we "cleaned up the ingredients."

And just like that, our customers got exactly what they wanted: great-tasting, affordable food with only clean ingredients listed on the labels. As predicted by Jason, the customers loved the tastes of the new meals and they loved what they read on the label—and, of course, they never questioned how the new meals tasted so delicious with such clean ingredients.

The business was approaching its fourth birthday, but thanks to Jason, and because we were continually erasing and redrawing the line in the sand, my own company had become unrecognizable to me.

By then, the color-coded weight-loss system I'd designed had become completely useless, nothing more than a flashy gimmick to attract customers. It wouldn't work if the nutrition guidelines weren't being applied to the meals. Instead of customers calling to enthusiastically report that they'd lost an insane amount of weight, they were calling with questions about why they'd been putting on the pounds using our weight-loss program. Of course I knew the reason: they'd been eating cheese, butter, salt, and excessive amounts of sugar without realizing it.

This was the end of the "Lose seven pounds in seven days" phenomenon, though it wasn't the end of us promoting it. Quite the opposite, we doubled and tripled down on this marketing claim. Jason viewed this as a selling ploy. "This is perfect! Every time customers call to complain that they didn't lose the advertised weight, that's an opportunity for us to sell them something else." Just like I'd learned all that time ago from Weight Watchers.

After a few months of these changes I was no longer stopping to think, *Oh gosh! If I spread the message that such and such food is good for you—even though I've got no science to back it up, that it could have negative effects on people's health!* I wasn't thinking about the bigger picture of how my decisions were impacting the people eating our food; I was just focused on my job, focused on our bottom line.

13

FEELING INVINCIBLE: MONSANTO RUNS THE DEPARTMENT OF AGRICULTURE

Most days, at the sound of my alarm, I leaned over and kissed Brie, and made my way to the kitchen while trying not to trip over one of our four sphynx cats, which *insisted* on walking under my feet. I plopped salmon pâté onto their fancy china dish, grabbed my coffee, and ventured downstairs into my office. After checking on the day's numbers, I headed to the gym before swinging by the production kitchen to check in with Logan, and then headed to the prep kitchen.

I filled my first Big Gulp of the day as I prepared my meeting points for that morning's Google Hangout with the team during which I would talk for twenty minutes or so while everyone pretended to listen, then Jason would ignore and override me. A faint buzz was 100 percent necessary during these meetings. After the videoconference, I could hear the B-team piling in the door in the next room as I filled my second Big Gulp and began my calls for the day.

I pulled my sales scripts up on my computer screen, even though I knew them by heart, and I printed out my call list with each person's name, company name, address and time zone, their nutrition philosophy—paleo, vegan, bodybuilding, etc.—the current vendors they're working with, their background, and any other personal information I was able to find.

One particular day, I had a follow-up call with fitness model Linda Durbesson down in Florida; I was about to gain access to her vast fan base of millions of followers, most of whom were young men who didn't give a damn about eating healthy. The reason they were valuable to me, however, was because they would listen to anything Linda told them to do. Check out her profile on Instagram or Facebook and you'll understand why. I don't think I've ever seen a picture of her that didn't feature a close-up of her ass in a thong. She's fully aware that that's why people flock to her, and she doesn't care so long as they keep sending her money.

Signing her up had been a long and arduous process. On top of her wanting to talk for hours on end every time we spoke, she had only moved to America from France a couple of years before, and her English was broken at best. Surprisingly though, she knew tons of social media slang. She told me that having her own line of healthy meals would make all her model friends "jelly" and she agreed that Nutrisystem meals were "grotty," but that the samples I had sent her to taste were "on fleek." However, she struggled with phrases like "paragraph five of the contract" or questions such as "Do you have a tax ID?" And she was totally perplexed when I told her, "Gluten is bad here . . . people are afraid of it," to which she replied, "I don' understand. What *ees zees* gluteen you *menseon*?"

Next, I had a call with Eric Casaburi, the CEO of Retro Fitness—you might have seen him on an episode of *Undercover Boss*. He's a young ambitious guy who's always looking for an edge over his competition, and I wanted to be that edge. Then I had to follow up with Jeff Skeen, who used to own fifty-plus Gold's Gym locations before he sold them to start his own gym franchise called Fitness

Connection. After that, I had to sign and return the contract to Vic Sprouse, the CEO of Brickhouse Cardio Club, a relatively new fitness chain that already had sixty locations sprinkled across the country. Following that, I had a call with fitness celeb Amanda Russell and her manager. Amanda was YouTube's No. 1 next fitness guru, and she was always being featured in places like *Women's Health*, *Livestrong*, *Runner's World*, *Shape*, and *Forbes*. She also had a team of fitness coaches under her brand, so she was a very strategic partner for getting my food mentioned in all those places. After Amanda, I had one of my most important calls of the day with Richard Boyd over in California. Richard's the vice president of 24 Hour Fitness, the largest privately owned fitness chain in the United States, with four hundred twenty-five locations.

While I was on the phone, trying to decipher Richard's strong Australian accent, one of the cooks swung the office door open, nervously waving his hand to indicate that my attention was desperately needed in the kitchen. I held my finger up.

"Hey, Richard, they're calling for me in the kitchen. Would you mind if I give you a shout back later on?"

"No worries, mate. Some days it can be quite a bugga's muddle *ova'eah* too," which I could only assume meant a clusterfuck. "Just give us a holla *tomorra*."

I popped my head into the kitchen to see Babs cutting out chunks of her hair with scissors while screaming at Chef Kevin. I grabbed the scissors out of her hand and asked what was going on. Apparently, she had been trying to impersonate my playful morning greetings to him, and after several unsuccessful attempts at telling her to fuck off, he decided to spit his gum into her baseball cap sitting on the counter.

To separate them, I sent Babs to the salon next door, owned by Sir Thomas, a hairstylist friend of mine. I'd met him through the Miss America organization, because he did the hair and makeup for a lot of the pageant women, which meant he knew how to work with overly stressed people on the verge of a nervous breakdown. I asked him what kind of miracle he might possibly be able to pull off with Babs's chewing-gum debacle. Then I went back and told Kevin he owed her the cost of the haircut *and* a new hat, and, for my own amusement, switched his death metal Sirius channel to the most twangified country station I could find and locked the controls.

Twenty minutes later, there was a knock on my office door. "Come in!"

"Hey, Jeff, how are you?"

"Big Mike! What's going on, man?! Are you going to be ready for the stage, in what, eight, nine weeks?"

"That's actually what I wanted to talk with you about. I'm not sure I'm going to be able to compete."

"What are you talking about? A lot of people have you picked to win the whole thing; you've *gotta* compete."

"Yeah, I know, it's just that, with school and everything . . . I . . . I'm having a hard time with . . . supplies, ya know? The food, the supplements . . . and the, ya know."

"The what?"

"Well, ya know, to compete at that level, everyone's on Dbol."

"Oh! Right!" I felt guilty; bodybuilders using steroids was something we all knew but never spoke of, unless of course you used them too. "So how much are we talking here?"

"I hate to even ask, ya know . . . But everything's about seven hundred and fifty dollars a week all the way up until the show."

"Big Mike, you're an old friend, and I'm really pulling for you, so I'll tell you what: why don't I sponsor you, a thousand dollars a week until the show?" His eyes grew to twice their normal size. "And I'd really love it if after you win you accredited your success to our food, *which*, of course, I'll happily supply all of your steak and chicken, and all that too."

"Of course! I won't shut up about the food!"

I reached into my desk drawer and pulled out my safety-net envelope—I always kept five hundred dollars in cash for unexpected opportunities like this—and handed it to him.

"Here's a starter kit for you, but I need you to send me an email asking for official sponsorship, so I can send you the rest without you having to come in here each week. That way, it's all legit."

"You've got it! Thank you so much for this!"

"Not at all. I've got a scheduled call coming up in two minutes, but grab whatever you need out of the fridge on your way out. I'll be looking for your email."

With phone scripts, I didn't have to be in a good, focused sales mode in order to close a huge deal, because they made the sales process an automated numbers game. I predictably closed one out of five sales calls. So, after each chef meltdown, I returned to my office, refilled my mocha Zinfandel, and picked up right where I had left off.

In between my calls, I had to finish up the two magazine articles that were both due that day: "Why Personal Trainers Know More About Nutrition Than Doctors" and "Why Fake Sugar Is Better for You Than Real Sugar."

I had to wrap all of this up before lunchtime, because I had to be downtown to do two TV segments at noon—one live and one prerecorded, to be aired the following week. For that day's live segment, I showed viewers how we made our healthy chicken pomodoro—I had the chefs put everything together in advance so I could just BS my way through the recipe and then spend the rest of the time edutising the audience.

For the second segment, I explained the health benefits of drinking wine—the media never seems to get tired of hearing that—and at the end of the segment, I prompted the host to tell the viewers, "If you'd like to download a *free* copy of Jeff's latest book, go to such-and-such website." I didn't want viewers to go to my main website because, statistically, only a tiny fraction of them would have placed food orders. Instead, I aimed to funnel them into an IFS campaign so we could directly market to them. To that end, I sent them to what's known as an opt-in page that's designed specifically to offer visitors something they're interested in based on the TV segment they have just watched. You've probably been to one of these sites before, the ones that offer you something free, like an eBook, in exchange for your email address. This particular one was linked to an IFS campaign that immediately began marketing a recipe book, created by me, that matched wines to various healthy recipes because, obviously, I knew those viewers were specifically interested in healthy recipes and wine.

A week after the segment aired, once the back-end software confirmed the success of these two television-to-Infusionsoft campaigns, our coaches would then send my scripts from the two segments out to our list of health professionals so they could repeat them on the talk shows in their cities. Each one would send thousands of email addresses into our digital campaigns, and once all these potential customers had made a small leap for the free cookbook, the digital campaign would then start slowly and subtly soft-selling them their local fitness gurus' healthy meals, which I was producing.

Immediately after I recorded the second segment, I had to bolt across town, where I was giving a speech to a class of registered nurses at National Business College (now American National University). My talk was designed to implant specific talking points into these nurses' heads—things like "convenience, not willpower, is the key to weight loss" (translation: precooked, prepackaged meals are the key to weight loss) and "greater numbers equal a greater chance of success" (translation: get your girlfriends to sign up with you). The point was that the following week, while they were at the watercooler in the hospital cafeteria talking about how they're ready to get back on track and lose twenty pounds, these nurses would recall, *Maybe I'll try that guy's company, the one that makes all the food for you. But I don't want to be the only one. Will y'all do it with me?* Infiltrating nurses had become a regular strategy of mine. Not only were they almost as good as PTs at recommending my meals to their patients, but they were excellent customers themselves—they worked eighteen-hour shifts on their feet and didn't have time to make their own food.

My main job at the company was then marketing, molding the messages that we used to attract consumers to our food. But instead of marketing directly to consumers, since we were copacking our food under different names, my job was to create marketing material—press releases, articles, blogs, scripted lectures, and TV news segments—and then distribute them to the businesses selling our food so that it didn't seem like it was coming from us. This is where I learned all about edutising.

I was good friends with the corporate dietitian at one of the top three food retailers in the world—I believe *Fortune* had them ranked as number one in 2015. She showed me that if her objective was to promote products containing Stevia, for example, instead of running an advertisement for those products, she would put out a health tip to her customers saying something like, "Studies show that fake sweeteners are even worse than real sugar, so when you're buying your groceries this week, be sure to check the labels to make sure they're sweetened with all-natural Stevia." The point was that it didn't feel like an advertisement; viewers thought they had just learned something about nutrition, and it would stand out in their mind the next time they were shopping and saw the big "sweetened with all-natural Stevia" sticker on food labels.

"People don't fall for traditional advertising like they used to," she told me, "so instead of promoting the produce section, for example, we sell more produce by writing articles like '10 Foods That Help You Burn Fat While You Sleep,' '7 Foods to Avoid If You Want a Flat Stomach,' and 'A New Study Reveals 5 Lifesaving Superfoods.' The produce we've got on sale will subtly be suggested as these 'lifesaving superfoods.' And that's edutising."

"Ninety percent of all people on diets are women," my dietitian friend taught me, "so it should come as no surprise that we target them on purpose." There were three main methods that her company used to target women: "First, we play to their insecurities," she taught me. "'Your arms are too flabby; your thigh gap isn't big enough.' Another is playing to their desires: 'Men will notice you more, other women will be so jealous of you.' And the newest method," she said, "is to play to their feminism: 'You can do anything you set your mind to, so take your power back and start losing weight today.' The best-selling book *Skinny Bitch*," she enlightened me, "educates female consumers to think, 'Eating meat is bad for your health; go vegan instead!' And when women hear this message," she continued, "and they think they've learned about a healthier, cleaner way to eat—and on top of that feel sexy and empowered to take action. That's when they buy!"

She taught me how to create edutisements of my own and how to send them down the media rabbit hole. I started distributing them to personal trainers, dietitians, doctors, and bloggers, who turned around and submitted them to newspapers, magazines, news programs, and medical journals. I started seeing *my* edutisement messages showing up in *The New York Times*, *Men's Fitness*, and *Women's Fitness*, and all over TV—I had fitness experts sending me links to television segments across the country.

Edutising was powerful and cheap, and if you did it right, a message could grow legs really fast. Consumers had seemingly gone deaf to traditional advertising, but when they heard a reputable health expert repeat an edutisement, they were not only open to hearing the message, but passionately adopted it as their own. Did a message need to be backed by science? Did I need to research it first? Did I have to believe it myself? No. And just like with the talk show segments, our coaches took my speech transcript, along with a list of venues by zip code where RNs could be reached, and sent them to our fitness influencers so they could follow my formula and drive more RNs—in *your* city—to promote our food.

After my speech, I headed toward the production kitchen. During my commute, I conducted a Bluetooth teleconference with over a hundred of Jason and Aaron's franchisees. I trained them on the new edutisements I wanted them spreading to their clients and local community for the following month. I spent about ten minutes laying everything out in detail for them, then I opened up the line for ten minutes of questions, where they asked things like "What kind of percentage will I make on this?" and "What day of the month do you send out commission checks?" rather than "What's the science behind the health benefits of this?" or even "Will this help my clients lose weight?"

When I arrived at the kitchen, I wrapped up the conference call and put on my sales face for my meeting with Rico, the CEO of a protein cookie company who had flown in from Florida to discuss a potential partnership. He shipped me some samples of his product a few days before, along with all the specs—recipes, ingredient breakdown, labor costs, nutrition facts—and that day we would be going over all the details of me taking over his manufacturing, distribution, and back-end logistics. These are tough growth points for food companies, because they require a very detailed set of systems like the one I learned from McDonald's.

Distribution can be one of the trickiest elements to master because there are so many moving parts. Everything affects everything else: order size affects dry ice requirements, which, along with geography, affects transit time, which in turn affects days and times that orders need to be produced, packaged, and delivered. For example, if we were on the East Coast, and a retailer in Washington State placed an order on a Tuesday for two thousand meals, we had to switch from UPS to FedEx—we used both, but UPS only handles certain packages on Mondays—and FedEx needs to be notified to make an express pickup for Monday. The meals need to be prepared and frozen on Friday and packed in dry ice on Saturday afternoon—because if they sit too long, the dry ice evaporates over the weekend and there won't be enough to keep the food frozen on its cross-country trip.

I briefly explained all of this boring logistical shit to Rico— capturing and converting website orders into detailed packing slips, producing accurate and timely shipping labels that matched the packing slips, the inventory and purveyor delivery schedule, affiliate tracking software, the bookkeeping system for commission payouts, and up-to-date P&L spreadsheets to track all of it. I could tell by the way Rico's eyes glazed over after the first sentence that this guy needed my help if he wanted to grow.

After I took him on a tour of the kitchen, I chauffeured him over to the prep kitchen, so he can try the mock samples of his cookies that the B-team had created for him, then asked Babs to transport Rico back to the airport, so I could begin preparing for the biggest part of the day: my performance that evening.

I was hosting another one of my own events, at which I supplied the food and entertainment. I checked in with Brie, then my official event manager, to make sure everything was ready to go: the food and drinks would be arriving on time, we had the correct number of seats set up, the sound system and microphone headset were properly tested, all of our vendor spots were sold, and all the attendees had been followed up with to confirm their arrival.

I had to be onstage in twenty minutes.

Brie and I had been promoting this big event, hosted at a fancy country club in the heart of downtown, for about a month, and we had sold 200 seats—not our biggest crowd. "Hormones, Wine, and Weight Loss" was the sexy name. We began with a wine tasting, and for hors d'oeuvres, I had the B-team prepare a menu of their choosing. The majority of them were thrilled at the opportunity to put their culinary skills to work without the hindrances of profit margins or having to keep mass scale logistics in mind.

Babs concocted an amazing recipe for cauliflower cheddar fritters, which I knew would be a huge hit, and her mini smoked salmon pizzas with light cream cheese seemed like a perfect palate cleanser before switching from a fruity red to a dry white. Kevin's entrées, however, aimed for the moon. The artistry of his spicy hoisin-glazed turkey meatballs paired with horseradish-crusted eggplant french fries—the ones that caused Babs to cut open her hand on TV—were surely underappreciated. And his herb-and-citrus leg of lamb paired with garlic-roasted brussels sprouts and olive-almond relish was the kind of talent best suited for nose-up cuisine connoisseurs. When unchained, this son of a bitch could really put on a culinary show.

The only crew member who didn't love this project was Craigslist Casey, and unfortunately for him, two hours after the rest of the staff had gone home to get dolled up for the event, he was still working, because he showed up to work two hours late.

After I'd coiffed my hairdo to perfection, I hopped into my car, turned the key, and . . . nothing. I pounded a fist against the steering wheel. The Extortion Cougar had emptied my fucking tank, *again*, and also poured out the portable backup that I so asininely had left in the passenger seat with the car's top down.

I had to do the unthinkable: I had to ask Casey for a favor. "I'm running late and I've got to be onstage in a few minutes; I need to borrow your car."

I'm sure he'd sooner have given up porn and sports and actually have begun asserting himself at work before doing me any favors, but he lacked the marbles to tell me no, so with a red face, he reached into his pocket and dropped his keys into my palm.

When I opened the door to Casey's beat-up Accord, I was punched in the nose by an overwhelming blend of cigarette smoke from the two overflowing ashtrays and Cool Ranch from the crumpled bags of Doritos leaking into the passenger seat. I turned the key and nothing happened. I realized that I had to blow into the ignition interlock device before his car would start, so I used the bottom of my shirt to wipe any remnants of Casey's saliva from the mouthpiece, and scrunched my face as I sealed my lips over the plastic straw and exhaled as hard as I could.

The device beeped, accompanied by a red light to inform me that I'd failed.

It hadn't even crossed my mind that I had been drinking; drinking had become another involuntary bodily function to me, like breathing or selling. Of course, upon failing, the Ignition Interlock Device immediately sent a signal to the authorities notifying them that the owner of the car had attempted to drive while under the influence. This meant that Casey would then get to keep his ignition-starting Breathalyzer for another six months. *Dick move, Jeff, dick move.* Casey's face practically turned maroon when I handed his keys back and told him the news.

Luckily, Babs was just getting back from dropping off Rico at the airport, so I asked her to drive me over to the event. Now that we were running behind, I told her that she didn't have time for luxuries like stopping for stop signs or yielding to any pedestrians audacious enough to use crosswalks while we were running late. As Babs sped down the road, I triple-checked my jacket pocket to make sure I had my fancy pen—that night's event had a very important mission.

In 2010, Monsanto, which was fighting with the FDA over approval of its genetically engineered growth hormone, took over Washington. If you don't follow this stuff closely, you probably didn't notice what President Obama did as soon as he got into office: he immediately appointed the former director of Monsanto, Roger Beachy, as director of the National Institute of Food and Agriculture (a department within the USDA), and former Monsanto lobbyist Islam Siddiqui as the new agriculture trade representative. But the craziest of all was his appointment of Monsanto's legal strategist and vice president for public policy, Michael Taylor, as the FDA's deputy commissioner. Taylor bounces back and forth between government agencies and Monsanto positions like a hand-stamped bar hopper on his twenty-first birthday—1976, 1991, 1994, 1996, and 2009, to be specific. After Monsanto infiltrated the government, of course, the FDA approved its genetically modified growth hormone.

It fascinated the hell out of me that a company could wield so much influence over our elected officials.

There was something important I wanted to do via political means too, and although I didn't exactly have Monsanto's lobbying power, I *did* have a strong presence in my community and the ability to rally and influence people. First, I joined a couple of city council boards so that I could directly weigh in on public policies, began endorsing organizations like the Chamber of Commerce, and then started organizing community events—like that night's event— where I would draw impassioned crowds and rally their support to ban unhealthy foods and keep our city healthy.

———

When we arrived at the venue, a sea of well-dressed guests swarmed to greet me, and Brie started miking me up—while giving me hell for showing up at the last minute—as I glad-handed my way to the front of the room and began my presentation. After sharing a handful of galvanizing anecdotes punctuated with a few key health industry statistics, I'd built up to the action-packed climax of my performance: the scale smash.

After I finished my speech, I had the audience stand up and form a giant circle around the bathroom scale lying in the center of the floor. While everyone was staring at the scale in curiosity, I reached behind my podium and pulled out my Louisville Slugger. With the bat tucked in my armpit, I began smacking my hands together and the crowd quickly began to join me. Once I felt the volume in the room was loud enough to terrify the dinner banquet in the next room, I extended the bat to the first volunteer—naked Tom, my old client from Fit Studio, now fully clothed—and had everyone cheer him on as he went to town on the scale. Springs and levers flew through the air as hundreds of applauding onlookers shouted at the top of their lungs. After naked Tom vented his passion, he then offered the bat to Libby, who then offered it to no-underwear Carrie, and then to diabetes-free Joy. After a few dozen volunteers had taken their turn at the bat, the scale had been obliterated into hundreds of pieces of cheap plastic and metal debris scattered across the floor. Our message was powerful: We're fed up with America's obesity epidemic, and we're going to do something about it!

Once their emotions were high, I gave them their instructions.

"Now, as you all just felt," I shouted, "it's easy to lift a baseball bat. But if you want to make *real* change, it's going to require you lifting a much more powerful weapon." I pulled my fancy pen from my jacket pocket. "Tonight, I need you to lift this," I said as I held the pen up for everyone to see. "*This* is how real change happens." Then I reached back to the podium and grabbed a clipboard. On the clipboard was a petition.

"Our city has been working on a bill that will allow unhealthy food vendors—hot dog stands, to be specific—to flood our down-town streets. Our elected officials want to bombard us with cheap, shitty, quasiconsumable sustenance that would be passed off as food—*I'm not having it*! By signing your name to this petition I'm holding in my hand: we have the power to prevent these assholes from infiltrating *our* city."

I set the clipboard on top of the podium and signed my name at the top for everyone to see.

"I'm going to take the video of tonight's scale smash," I said as I pointed to the video crew at the back of the room, "and I'm going to send it along with this petition full of signatures to our city council members to tell them we don't want these vendors bringing their shit food into our community, and if they don't care enough about us to support this cause, we *will* vote them out of office. That's the message we're going to send them—that is," I said as I extended my pen to the nearest audience member, "if you all join me."

I roused the room back into a passionate cheer as the clipboard got passed around, and each person was applauded as he or she scribbled a signature down. When the clipboard made its way back to me, it had two hundred names added to it.

After the event, Brie stayed behind to close everything down, so Babs took me to fill my portable tank and then dropped me off at my car. I was too energized to head straight home, so I decided to go for a drive with the windows down in the cool evening breeze. I was in my own little world as I glided around all my favorite places in the city—down Jefferson Street in front of the giant, golden Wells Fargo Tower, along Gainsboro Road to see the PGM-19 Jupiter Rocket (previously an active nuclear warhead that Roanoke purchased from the US government, for some reason), and up Walnut Street, underneath the Roanoke Star, lit up in all its glory. After such an electrifying and successful event, I was in too great of a mood to have let anything get me down—not even the police officer who had just pulled behind me with his red-and-blues flashing.

"License and registration," he said sternly.

"Here you go."

"Do you know why I pulled you over this evening?"

"Yeah, you looked bored sitting on the side of the road, so I thought I'd run that red light and give you something to do." He chuckled as he gave my license a once-over. "That's a pretty good one."

He then turned to walk back to his car so he could run my plates, and I decided to take a chance. "Hey, I'll make you a deal, man: If you let me off with a warning, I promise I won't finish the rest of my six-pack until I get home." The officer bent over, puts his hands on his knees, and began laughing harder than I'd ever seen a policeman laugh.

"I've *never* heard that one before." He held out my license. "Here, take this and get out of here."

I was feeling invincible.

I headed back to the prep kitchen to make myself a nightcap before driving the rest of the way home. On my way there, as a small, apologetic gesture for the Breathalyzer incident, I swung by a store and picked up a rather ironic gift for Casey: a case of his favorite lager. I put a bow on it and a little card with an enclosed hundred-dollar bill to hopefully cover the cost of recalibrating his IID device.

At the kitchen, I filled my Big Gulp with a dry red. After I downed the last sip, I looked out the window into the parking lot to make sure it was Cougar-free, then headed home.

When I got to the house, Brie was sitting up in bed with the computer on her lap, wearing nothing but my T-shirt, chatting on her Bluetooth with someone about an upcoming event that I was being requested to speak at. I quietly began her nightly foot massage, which graduated into a back massage after she hung up the phone. I told her what an amazing job she did with the event, that I couldn't have done it without her, and how much I loved and adored her.

14

YES, WE'RE MAKING PEOPLE FAT, BUT WE'RE NOT GOING TO DO ANYTHING ABOUT IT

Brie and I both had a decent buzz going as our plane touched down in the Dominican Republic. When we got to the resort, our personal concierge, Mario, greeted us, put drinks in our hands, and walked us up to our suite. Each day in the Dominican Republic was like a fairy tale. We never wanted to leave. On our last day, Brie put up a good fight to stay an extra week, but I came up with a convincing reason why we should return to the States: I asked whether she wanted to buy a house in Florida, so that we could always be near the beach. I desperately needed to get out of the 'burbs. She was so excited she immediately began calling agents and scheduling walk-throughs.

The next day, when our plane touched down in Miami, we rented a car and drove to Tampa, where we had three houses to tour. I went on the first two tours; the first place was OK, but every room was carpeted, even the bathroom, but the second place seemed like a winner: high ceilings, a giant kitchen that Brie was obsessed with, a screened-in sunroom, where the cats could soak up rays all day, and a balcony that overlooked the giant swimming pool in the court-yard. When we got to the third tour, I pretended to receive an im-portant call from Jason so that I could sneak off for an hour. Our four-year anniversary—which also meant the company's fifth-year anniversary—was only two months away. Brie's hints were becoming increasingly less subtle, but I didn't want to rush the proposal.

I was booked to give one of my nutrition performances the weekend before our anniversary, and for the grand finale, we would be doing a "cupcake toss," a fun and messy game in which my helpers walked around giving out handfuls of Little Debbie cakes to audi-ence members, who then hurled them across the room into Dump-sters for prizes as their shouting peers rooted them on. I'd already made sure that Brie's mother was going to be in the audience, though I hadn't told her the real reason why. "You haven't been to one my events yet, Janice, and it would really mean a lot to me if you were there."

After everyone else had had their turn, I would draw the crowd's attention to me as I took Brie's hand. We would step *waaay* back, to make the toss seem impossible. Then I would up the stakes. "If I make this," I would tell the audience, "everyone here gets a free week of meals on me." I would take the cupcake in my hand and wind my arm way, way back, to draw attention away from my other hand, reaching into my jacket pocket. Then, right as I'd be about to make the toss, I would "accidently" drop the cupcake and bend down on one knee to pick it up, but instead of lifting the cupcake off the ground, I would hold up the ring to Brie as I popped the question in front of everyone.

Brie's heart would melt, the women in the audience would "aww," and after she would undoubtedly say yes, I would snatch up the cup-cake and alley-oop it to a helper, who would slam-dunk it so I could give everyone the week of free meals.

It was going to be perfect.

It had been two weeks since my last conference call, and as I stood in my office at the prep kitchen, filling my giant coffee mug, I was hoping that our vacation to the Dominican Republic served as a reset button so I could once again handle those meetings with an air of decorum, but three minutes into a call, Jason was already testing my patience.

"I think that—"

"If we just—"

"Oh, sorry, go ahead."

"No, you go."

. . . Long pause . . .

I filled my shot glass and leaned out of my iPad's camera range, tilted my head back to toss the fiery clear liquid down my throat, and popped back into view.

"Like I was saying—"

"Why don't we—"

"My bad."

"Sorry, what were you going to say?"

. . . Long pause . . .

"*OK, listen!*" I said to break the cycle. "We need to get this figured out! What do you plan to do?" I asked, though I knew he couldn't have cared less. "We need to solve this issue of our customers' gaining weight."

"We at FCG," he began puking out his diplomatic bullshit, "pride ourselves in being a company that 'gives a shit' about everyone we work with, so I'm sure we can find a way to solve this issue." *Let me guess, you also plan to cut taxes, create jobs, and stimulate the economy.*

I couldn't stand Jason's lack of sympathy toward our clients. I was getting calls from longtime customers telling me how much weight they'd been gaining and how disappointed they were. He didn't care. He never interacted with these people. To him, our customers were just numbers on a spreadsheet, and their importance was determined by the number of zeros beside their names.

"OK . . . Well, would you like to explore any solutions?"

"I can't think of any," Jason said lethargically. "Do you have any in mind?"

"Well, yeah. If we're not willing to change the ingredients—"

"We're not."

"I *get* that! So since we're not willing to change the ingredients, we need to at least offer a subsidiary line of meals that don't have any seasoning on them; a naked line that customers can either eat as is or season themselves."

"No."

"What do you mean no?"

"No, we're not going to waste resources on a second line of food that stands no chance of competing with our main line. The cost won't justify the ROI. We'd have to hire more cooks, create new procedures, order twice as much from our purveyors—no."

"Well, then." I opened the discussion to everyone else on the call. "Can anyone else think of any possible ways to help our customers?"

"I think a better use of our time today would be to discuss the bugs on the website."

Vodka shot.

I let out a sigh intended to be heard. "What about the goddamn website, Jason?"

"It's not upselling the customers based on their choices, for some reason, and, Jill—correct me if I'm wrong—you've gone through the code and can't find the source of the glitches, right?"

"Correct," she replied.

"So, let's break this down," I suggested, "If the site is tracking customers based on their URLs—"

"Wait a minute," Jason interrupted me, "I think you meant to say 'IP addresses.'"

"What's that, now?"

"The site," he corrected me, "tracks customers by their IP addresses, not the URLs—the URL is the thing they type into the box at the top of their browsers that brings them to our website."

"Fine," I told Jason, "the *IP address* is what the site uses to track customers. So, Jill, is there a way to set Infusionsoft to use the customers' cache to—"

"Cookies!" he corrected me again.

"Huh?"

"We need to track cookies, not the cache," he pointed out. "Cache is the thing on people's computers that remembers the sites they visit and helps them get back to those sites quicker."

"Jason! You know what I mean! What the fuck does it matter which word I use?! Here, let me be more clear: customers are getting *bamboozled* every time they visit our *doohickey* and try to click on one of the *doodads* at the top right side of the *thingamajig*! So we're going to need someone to fix the little *whatchamacallit* so that people can order those little *gizmo thingies* we sell. That better?"

Jason replied, "There's no need to be difficult, Philips."

I had to fight the compelling urge to spasm into a full-blown, body-shaking tantrum. I held it in and leaned to the side. Double vodka shot.

After another few minutes of arguing over terminology, the call ended with Jason saying, "Well, Philips, I trust you'll find a solution."

Vodka shot.

The day hadn't even begun yet and I already had a strong buzz setting in, so after the conference call, I went to the pantry and switched from vodka back to my coffee-wine mixture. Now that I'd started drinking, I couldn't stop or I'd have crashed; I just needed to ease up, until at least lunchtime, so I could last the day. The B-team would be walking through the door any minute, so I needed to hurry.

Babs was now injuring herself every single day, sometimes more than once. It was a shame, because she really was an enjoyable person to be around—she was funny and charismatic, and had a ton of potential if she could have just honed it in on something—but she was getting so much worse. She had been ruining so much food that she was costing me money. Everyone—Kevin, Casey, even Brie— had been telling me I should fire her, and that would have been the smart business move, but I had this inexplicable paternal feeling toward her.

About forty-five minutes into the day, Babs was applying a fresh bandage to the gash she had added to her finger collection the day before when the oven timer went off. "I've got it!" she shouted as she dashed toward the oven. On her way, she bumped into Cryin' Kevin, knocking the spatula out of his hand and naturally causing him to scream, "What the fuck?!" We all turned to see what he was whining about this time, and unable to react in time, I watched Babs reach into the four-hundred-degree oven and grab the two giant steaming trays of chicken with her bare hands. It took a second for the pain signal to travel from her hands to her brain, at which point she screamed at the top of her lungs and immediately dropped the trays to the floor, ruining about two hundred dollars' worth of meals.

Half irritated, half disappointed, I asked, "Goddamnit, Babs; are you OK?"

"I'm fine," she said as sniffled. "It just hurts really bad."

I wanted to say, "Of course it hurts. You grabbed a four-hundred-degree tray without hand towels, ya dumbass!" But at the sight of her tearful face, I resisted and, sighing, went through the Babs protocol. "OK, you know what to do: head into the office so we can document it. Kevin, quit your bitching and grab the first-aid kit for her."

This little mishap was going to leave us short on the latest focus group orders shipping out that day, which meant that someone would have to drive out to the distribution center to pick up more chicken.

Since we only needed a couple of cases of chicken, I opted to take my own car, and to my surprise, when I turned on the ignition, there was still half a tank of gas!

The quickest route to the US Foods hub was to go all the way down Main Street, and even though my gas tank hadn't been struck yet that day, the Extortion Cougar had been hunting me with tenacity lately. I decided to take back roads. It was a gorgeous day: blue, cloudless sky, mild temperature.

I turned left onto Kimball and then immediately right as I

maneuvered the forty-five-degree angle that wrapped around the giant church on the corner. Midturn, something caught my eye: an old man in overalls about a dozen yards away staring at me with his hands on his cheeks and a terrified look on his face. He was staring at a big black object rolling right at him. I squinted into the sun.

Just as I realized it was my wheel, the front of my car slammed down into the pavement, and I skidded across the asphalt. A wave of sparks flew.

Once the car skidded to a halt, I looked back to see my wheel—the entire rim with a tire on it—rolling across the street, where the old man intercepted it.

I made my way around the car; the back two wheels looked normal. But when I got to the front passenger side, my stomach dropped. The front passenger side wheel was still intact, but there were no lug nuts on it.

I had no way to prove it, but the Cougar was pissed that she was losing her power over me and wanted to teach me a lesson.

The old man rolled my wheel over to me and helped me take three of the six lug nuts off the back two wheels and apply them to the front two.

"It's a good thing I wasn't on Main Street, huh?" I asked the old man.

"You better be thankful you weren't on the interstate."

I couldn't go to the police to report a driving incident with vodka on my breath. I couldn't bring myself to come clean with Brie. I didn't know what to do.

The Cougar was a problem, but she wasn't the biggest problem I was facing at the moment. It seemed like every day another customer was calling my cell phone to tell me how upset they were because of the weight they'd mysteriously gained while eating my food. These weren't faceless voices on the phone; these were longtime clients of mine—close friends and family members. The one that really killed me was Quinton, the guy from Atlanta who'd lost one hundred forty pounds. He hadn't gained it *all* back, but he was upset with me, and even worse, he was back to hating himself again. I felt awful. My company had gone from performing weight-loss miracles to taking advantage of people's trust of me and my food.

When I got back to the kitchen with the cases of chicken, I told the B-team that there was a change of plans: "The other kitchen will still be used for making the shitty line of food, and you guys will now be making the quality meals that we'll ship out of here, just like we used to." The next day, I contacted as many customers as I could and filled them in on the situation. "We've now got a newer, even healthier line of meals, guaranteed to help you lose the recent weight you've gained—I give you my word—but the only way to order them is through me, over the phone." By the end of the day, I'd brought in a little over eight thousand dollars' worth of food orders, the next day, fourteen thousand, and twenty thousand the day after that.

Brie and I were returning from Florida again. After having toured a few more places, we'd selected our Tampa house-to-be and set the moving date at four weeks from our anniversary (my surprise proposal day), which was coming up the following weekend. We were walking through the airport, getting ready to catch our flight back to Virginia, when my phone buzzed with a call from Jason. For the first time since we'd met, I had a good feeling in my stomach about a conversation with him.

I answered with a smile. "What's up, Jason? Are you calling to thank me for the revenue spikes?"

"I think it's best if we part ways," he said in a surprisingly mellow tone.

Those eight glorious words were the most benevolent gift he could have possibly given me—a way out of our corporate marriage—but before I jumped for joy, I needed to confirm that I'd heard him right. "Just to make sure I understand, I found a way to bring in extra money this past week and now you want to liquidate our partnership?"

"I saw the bank account, yes, but you did it behind our backs."

"I had to," I said coolly. "You said no when I asked you to make the meals actually work for our customers again."

"Being a team player is one of the top things I look for in a partner."

"How am I *not* a team player? I brought you extra money and it didn't even cost you the up-front investment you were worried about." Then I realized I was playing defense when I should have shut my mouth, grabbed the ball, and sprinted. "But you're right. I shouldn't have done it without your permission, so I understand."

"So, then, I'm going to have our attorneys send you some paperwork in a couple of days, and if you can get everything signed and emailed back to me, we can work on the asset allocation."

I couldn't believe how well this was going. He was being uncharacteristically agreeable. Come to think of it, that *was* the best conversation I ever had with Jason! I felt like giving the cold, calculating dickhead a hug through the phone.

"We'll need to spend the next couple of weeks signing the necessary papers and letting our affiliates, our retail locations, our employees, and our customers know about the situation."

He ended the conversation with "No hard feelings, buddy. Sometimes partnerships just don't work out."

"I couldn't agree more!" I probably fired back a little too enthusiastically.

Once we got on the plane, Brie was terrified of flying and couldn't find her Xanax, so she had her face buried in her lap trying to forget that she was miles above the ground.

I, however, couldn't stop fidgeting in my seat the entire flight; there was too much to think about. The second we touched the ground, I would call Logan and begin adjusting the ingredients back to the way they were, then I needed to find someone to make the adjustments to the website, after which I would send a mass email to our customers to let them know that change was coming—good change. *Oh, and we need to run a huge celebratory special, some giant discount!* I couldn't type the notes fast enough into my phone.

When the seat belt light came on, I switched my phone off

airplane mode and it immediately started buzzing. A series of texts came through from my social media guy, Dex. He was technically an independent contractor, even though his paychecks came from FCG, instead of our joint company, but he was a good friend and my mole inside the system, who always kept me up to date. According to his messages, Jason had begun shutting down all of our systems. He told me Jason had shut down the website, which meant the customers had no way of placing orders. He had shut down Infusionsoft, which meant I had no access to our customer database. They had shut down our credit card merchant service and our bank account, which meant that even if I could have gotten a hold of them, I had no way of accepting our customers' money.

He told me that our bookkeeper—*their* bookkeeper, actually—wouldn't be sending out checks anymore, which meant that my employees, my purveyors, and FedEx and UPS wouldn't be getting paid anymore. Also, my online affiliates—who made up roughly half of all the sales—wouldn't be receiving their commission checks, and I don't know too many salespeople who enjoy working for free. Possibly worst of all, I was blacklisted me from the FSE. Apparently no one in Jason sphere of influence was to do business with me moving forward. I still had control of the kitchen, but what good was that if there weren't any orders to fill.

I was out.

I had heard rumors that Jason had done something like this to a previous partner—stripping all of the digital assets and leaving nothing but physical overhead and debt—but Jason was so cordial on the phone I assumed it wasn't going to happen to me. It was a pretty shrewd move on his part. I didn't know what to think. I was in complete shock.

That afternoon, all money movement, in and out of the company, had come to a halt. The very account that I paid myself from was frozen and inaccessible to me. The next day, production had to be shut down.

15

ALL ALONE, SHIRTLESS, WEARING HANDCUFFS

I wasn't looking forward to the conversations I was about to have. First, I would have to tell Logan, who would handle the dirty work at the production kitchen for me. Then I would personally have to tell the B-team that they were being let go. It was Friday, and I'd given everyone the day off, since there wasn't anything for them to do.

I asked Casey, Kevin, and Babs to meet me at the kitchen, and spread their meeting times far enough apart that I would have time between each one to muster up my courage. I started with Casey.

He made my job a little easier when he came in forty-five minutes late. I invited him into the office, and when he walked in, I didn't beat around the bush.

"Casey, I'm sorry to tell you, you're being let go, man."

His face turned bright red. "Why, what did I do?"

"Frankly, lots of stuff—but that's got nothing to do with it. Everyone's being let go. We're shutting down."

"I can't believe this is how you do me," he said, his lower lip protruding as he spoke, "after all I've done for you."

"I don't want to talk about it, Casey."

"I can't believe this is how you treat someone who helped you grow your company," he said as his lip trembled. He was right. I felt horrible.

"Casey, you're a good guy," I felt compelled to tell him. "It's . . . nothing . . . personal," which was mostly true. "We're just shutting down, man. I need your key."

He took it off his keychain and handed it to me, then walked out the door.

I wasn't looking forward to telling Kevin, not because I couldn't handle his verbal abuse, but because he was a genuinely good guy when you looked deep down—deep, *deep* down—and I was worried about what this might do to his already shattered self-esteem. I took a couple of vodka shots before inviting him into the office, and when he walked through the door, I bulldozed right through it. "Hey, Kevin, I'm sorry to say we're shutting down this kitchen operation. I've got to let everyone go. You didn't do anything wrong. It's just the way it is."

He looked me square in the eyes for the first time ever and said, "It's all good man," then a hint of a smile crept onto the corner of his mouth. "I never liked working in this shit hole, anyway."

I laughed. "Exactly! So, consider this your Christmas present from me."

"Hey," he offered, "if you want me to, I'll stay through the end of the day and help clean this place up."

"Sure! That would be great man." I patted him on the shoulder. "You're a good guy."

"Fuck off, you emotional Care Bear motherfucker."

"Ha! There's the Kevin I'll miss."

But Babs was going to be much harder. The more I thought about it, the more unsure I felt. I was worried about her. I felt like I had to find something for her to do. Maybe she could be my traveling assistant for a while, help me with my speeches; maybe I could get her a job working for Manny—*something*.

Ten o'clock rolled by, ten-thirty, and then eleven o'clock—no

Babs. It wasn't like her to show up late, at least not without calling to let me know she had to make an emergency stop at a car wash and detail her car. Something was off. I sent a text to see whether everything was OK with her—no reply.

A few minutes after noon, I was sitting in my office talking on the phone when I heard the blast of the kitchen door slamming against the wall in the next room. I walked into the kitchen to see Hurricane Babs making a mess, dropping things all over the floor, avoiding eye contact with me, packing her personal equipment into a giant bag. "Babs . . ." I said, "what's going on?"

"Oh, like you don't know," she bellowed.

"I *don't* know—that's why I'm asking you," I said. "You seem upset about something."

"I am upset! I want to know why I'm not working today!"

"Well, that's what I wanted to talk with you abou—"

"If you're going to fire me," she interrupted as she continued to frantically grab her equipment off the counter and slam it into her bag, "the right thing to do is to tell me to my face."

"Babs, I'm not firing you. Yes, we're shutting down both kitchens and everyone else is being let go, but I was actually going to ask *you* whether you—"

"Whatever, Jeff. I thought you were different!" Then she began crying. "I thought I . . ." She gasped a few times. "I could trust you!"

"Babs, please, listen; I'm offering y—"

"I don't want you to call me begging me for help ever again! And I don't want you using any of the recipes I created in here, either! And you can't fire me, because I fucking quit!" I let her rant on for a minute, spit flying from her lips as she screamed at me. "You're selfish; you never cared about me!" Then she stomped her foot on the ground. "I hope I never see you again, ever!"

After she'd gotten everything out of her system, she stormed out the door, and rather than chasing after her, I realized she had just done the very thing that I had lacked the fortitude to do myself—she fired herself.

Later that evening, I was sitting in my office, drinking alone, when I got a call from Babs. She wanted to know why she was being fired. I reminded her that I hadn't fired her; she had made an incorrect assumption and quit. She said she changed her mind and wanted a job, and then hung up the phone before I could respond.

About ten minutes later, she showed up back at the kitchen, thankfully with her roommate (a witness), and began screaming in my face. I kept my mouth shut during her sobbing diatribe, which apparently enraged her further. As she continued shouting, she began running around the room, picking random objects up—salt and pepper shakers, a spatula, an egg timer, a frying pan—and hurling them at me as her moral supporter stood in the doorway, screaming at her to stop. After she had run out of utensils, her roommate finally came into the kitchen to grab her and guide her out the door. Babs tried turning back to continue screaming at me, but her roommate served as a barrier while she ushered the writhing wrecking ball across the parking lot.

I was heartbroken at the spectacle I'd just witnessed. Babs was the furthest thing from a bad person; she was just—*mistakenly*—spiritually crushed. I felt like calling her and trying to explain what was happening one more time and inviting her to come back.

I sat at my desk and downed four vodka shots as I stared at my phone contemplating for a minute. Then a fifth, and then a sixth shot. And after thoroughly thinking the situation through, I called a locksmith instead.

Before then, it hadn't yet sunk in that my business had been swept out from under me. No calls to make or answer, no schedules or meetings, no road trips or to-do lists, no food shipping out, no money coming in. What finally made me realize that it was all over were the chefs. They had been around since almost the very beginning. They'd helped me grow my business from me cooking chicken breasts on my George Foreman grill in my condo kitchen to a mass production company shipping food to every state in the country. I had just fired them all.

I'd read somewhere that the fifth year was the point at which most new businesses either succeeded or failed, and as I sat there staring at my blurry-looking desk, I couldn't help noticing that, sure enough, right at my five-year anniversary, I had failed. Sadness isn't what I felt though. I was way too numb for that. "So this chapter of my life is over—no biggie," I calmly acknowledged to myself. "And besides, tomorrow at the end of my speech," I cracked a big smile, "is going to be the perfect start to my new life, in Florida, with Brie as my fiancée."

It was the morning of the big day, and there simply wasn't enough alcohol in the house to help settle the roller coaster of emotions whirling through my head.

I was in the downstairs bathroom, fixing my hair and taking shots of vodka. I threw on my blazer and ran my hand across my heart; I felt the little circle with the stone in my pocket. A wave of nerves was rushing through me. The vodka shots I'd taken over the previous ten minutes were kicking in and I was feeling a very euphoric high. I practically levitated up the stairs, my invisible cape waving in the wind as I floated down the hallway—though still tripping over the four meowing sphynxes walking under my feet—on my way to find Brie.

As I reached for the doorknob, I felt like I was going to explode. I could barely hold in my little secret. I wanted to pop the question right there and then. I took a deep breath and tried talking some sense into myself.

I opened the door and saw Brie kneeling on the ground, pulling clothes from the bottom dresser drawer, and cramming them into a suitcase.

"Uh, babe . . . we've still got a few weeks before we need to pack for Florida."

No response.

"Are you about ready to head over to the event?"

Without lifting her head to look at me, she drily replied, "I'm not going."

Completely confounded, I asked, "Is something wrong? Why aren't you going?"

She continued packing as she responded, "I'm not going to any events anymore."

My invisible cape stopped blowing in the wind.

"What do you mean? I need you there. You helped set up this whole thing."

She dropped another handful of clothes into her bag and lifted her head to look at me. Showing no emotion, she said, "I'm leaving," then sat still for a minute, staring into my eyes to gauge my response.

A lump swelled up in my throat. "Wh—what?" I ran my hand across my heart pocket and swallowed the painful gulp. "Wh—what's going on?"

"I'm leaving," she said without blinking. "You're not going anywhere anymore. Everything around you is sinking, and I'm not going to drown with you."

I tried to convince her otherwise. "The business? That's just a small speed bump—you know I'll bounce right back."

"I don't think so," she shot me down.

"What?" I asked in disbelief. "You don't believe in me anymore?"

Without even the courtesy of hesitation, she confirmed my darkest fear, "No."

I felt like throwing up.

She zipped her suitcase, said she'd be back in a few days for the rest of her things, scooped up the sphynxes, and walked out the front door, leaving me in a cold, dark, shell of a home, with a useless ring in my pocket.

I had to be onstage within twenty minutes, but I felt like a salted slug.

After delivering what was truly the worst performance of my life, I didn't go out into the crowd to make small talk with everybody like I normally would; I just hid behind the stage until everybody was gone. I didn't want to see anyone. I didn't want them to see me.

With my head below my shoulders, I walked through the gigantic empty parking lot to my car. I just sat there. I couldn't hold a thought in my foggy, inebriated, serotonin-deficient head. I reached under the seat, grabbed my spare bottle of Sky vodka, and took a big sip.

I ran my hand across my heart again and felt the little circle in my pocket, then I took a few more big gulps of vodka, pulled the ring out, and tossed it across the parking lot. I couldn't stand to look at it.

I sat there in my car all afternoon, drinking. After catching a glimpse of my pathetic face in the rearview mirror, I ripped it off the windshield and tossed it into the parking lot, along with the ring.

I couldn't stop the movie reel of Brie walking out the front door from looping in my mind.

A homeless man toting a backpack walked along the sidewalk, and I found myself wondering what circumstances had brought him to where he was. Maybe he too had been very successful and run into a string of bad luck and bad decisions, landing him in destitution.

The sun was fading and my head was getting heavy.

I woke up sometime around two a.m., in a haze, and it took me a few minutes of reviewing the gigantic empty parking lot around me to remember where exactly I was and why I was there. Once my memory caught up, I decided that rather than walk five miles back to the house, it would be a fun game to see how far I could make it before the car died in the middle of the street.

I pulled out of the parking lot and began driving up the road, which had surprisingly heavy traffic for that time of night. I squinted and tried to focus on the taillights in front of me. *What the fuck is this guy driving so damn slow for?* I pounded the steering wheel. *Doesn't he know my tank is going to run out any minute now?!* In the side mirror, I noticed the pair of headlights getting way too cozy with my bumper; the guy behind me was riding my ass because of Sergeant Slow. I tried ignoring him for a mile or so, but he was *really* clinging to me.

I spun around to get a look at him, "*Go around!*" I shouted as I waved. "There's nothing I can do about it!"

Honk!

At the sound of a car horn in front of me, I whipped back around to realize I had crossed over the double yellow. I jerked the wheel back to my side of the road, barely missing the Camry flying in the opposite direction.

The interior of my car lit up like a blue-and-red strobe light.

I pulled off the side of the road, followed closely by my tailgating officer friend, who sternly asked for my license and registration.

"Let me help you out," I olive-branched him, "I *do* know what you pulled me for; I crossed the double yellow line. And yes, I was drinking—earlier—but that was quite a few hours ago." He then asked whether I would mind performing a few tests to prove I was capable of driving, and with the knowledge that alcohol simply didn't affect my motor skills, I agreed.

The officer started off with an easy one: I had to extend both of my arms straight out to the side with only my index finger poking out and hold them there while aiming my face upward toward the sky, then he would repeatedly call out either "left hand" or "right hand," to signal which finger I was to use to touch the tip of my nose without losing my balance.

"That the best you got?" I asked him.

Then he wanted to test my balance in motion, so he stepped about fifteen feet back and told me I had to walk a straight line to him, heel to toe every step, without breaking eye contact with him or losing balance.

"Easy peasy," I taunted him as I completed the task. "What else ya got?"

Then he got an interesting idea. "All right, Mr. Philips, I want you to say your ABC's without singing them."

Sounds easy enough, but since I hadn't recited my ABC's since kindergarten—where I was specifically conditioned to *sing* them— that took some serious effort, but I focused and pulled it off. I was doing just fine, but I was in the mood for a confrontation, and so, after the letter Z, I decided to tack on a smart-ass grand finale. Still in monotone, I said, "Now I've *said* my ABC's; next time won't you *say* them with me?" Needless to say, the officer wasn't amused.

"I'm going to need you to take a blow test," he said, and that's when I knew I was fucked. The policeman pulled his handcuffs out immediately after the device beeped to show I had blown a 0.18. Although more than double the legal limit, it was kind of amazing, because the liter bottle under my seat was empty.

I was tossed in the back of his car and taken to an empty holding cell, where I was told I would be kept until I sobered up enough to drive. The officer took my shirt, though he was kind enough to leave me the handcuffs, so that I wouldn't get too uncomfortable being able to move my arms around freely. I put my head down on the cold concrete bench, freezing my ass off, and lay awake.

PART III

16

TAKING VODKA SHOTS AT 5:30 AM, WITH STRANGERS ON A FLIGHT TO ISRAEL

The next month was a drunken, showerless haze.

I was also broke.

When Jason locked me out of our software and bank account, he'd left all of our purveyor and vendor accounts active, who, of course, had kept deducting money from the emptied business bank account. When it had gotten far enough below zero, Wells Fargo cleaned out my personal account to pay for it, but luckily I still had a few bucks in a separate credit union account.

With less than a hundred dollars to my name, my daily meals—when I remembered to eat—consisted of plain tuna straight from the can for breakfast and lunch. Dinner was bottom shelf vodka straight from the plastic bottle—having downgraded from Stoli to Skyy to Aristocrat. I didn't answer a single phone call for four weeks; friends, family, and the most caring of all, creditors—who were so concerned with my well-being that they tried their best to reach me six, seven times a day—were left to guess whether I was still alive.

The doorbell was constantly ringing. Flies were circling the trash can by the kitchen door. An untouched razor sat in the sink. And I was sporting a pit-stained T-shirt that doubled as a napkin. Depression was the only emotion I was capable of. Twenty pounds lighter, I lacked the strength to lift my head as I zombied from room to room through the empty house, hoping to find a feng shui that might break my mental funk. None of them did. The silence in the house was painfully deafening to me. Even though my depressive state made me antisocial, I was still yearning for some sort of casual interaction with someone—*anyone*—but I continued to ignore the phone calls.

Each day was a solitary, twenty-hour therapy session where I got to play both doctor and patient, and argued with myself over who was to blame for my situation. During my *less*-intoxicated moments—aka prebreakfast—I attempted finger-pointing at all the external causes.

Fucking USDA corruption and loopholes!
Fucking Jason and his constant revenue demands!
Fucking Craigslist Casey and his lethargic little smirks!
Fucking Cougar and her lecherous cat-and-mouse death games!
Fucking consumers and their incessant demands for cheap, shitty foods!
Fucking Nutrisystem!

Then, as the day would go on and the vodka in my veins increased, I would acknowledge the thing that I was too afraid to acknowledge sober, too disgusted to shine a light on until my nerves were sufficiently numbed: that over the past few years, I had become the very thing I despised most in this world.

"Oh, Jesus, no!" I slapped myself in the face. "How could I have let this happen?! How could I have let myself sink so low?!"

Early one morning, before I poured my first cup of vodka-diluted coffee, my phone buzzed with a text message from my sister. It said that she and her fiancé, Adam, had gotten plane tickets for a trip to

Israel and had a third one for me. Adam was a full-blown Jew, and my sister and I are half Jewish, on our mother's side.

At first, I ignored the text—responding would have put a damper on my morning self-loathing ritual—but after a dozen follow-ups, I felt she at least deserved a formal declination.

"Sounds like an amazing trip, but I'm going to have to sit this one out; I've got too much going on right now." I lifted my head off the floor to look around the empty room for my vodka bottle. "But you guys have a blast and take lots of pictures."

But she persisted on, "You need to Jew-up! This is a once-in-a-lifetime opportunity, and I'm not going to let you pass it up."

After five straight days of my rejections, she thought she would try a different approach: "We're going to be drinking the entire time we're there," she assured me, "and it's all on me." I began to pack.

The first thing we did when we got to JFK airport, as promised, was visit the duty-free shop, where we stocked up on the biggest bottles of each kind of liquor. The great thing about an international flight to Israel was that as we went through the TSA, there were special attendants for the Israel flight who came around and put our names and seat numbers on the bottles, so that once everyone was situated on the plane, the flight attendants could come around and issue our drinks back to us. No more than forty-five minutes into the twelve-hour flight, I watched three rows of millennials go from loud, obnoxious, shot-taking party animals to drooling, snoring vegetables. I chugged quickly so that I could join them.

Many hours later, I woke to someone tapping on my shoulder. Through blurry vision, I saw an old man with a thick beard and a single curly pigtail strand of hair dangling down each side of his face. He began walking toward the back of the plane, waving his hand as a signal for me to follow him. At the back of the plane, the man was standing with two other men dressed like him, in decorative robes, and holding briefcases with a black duffel bag at their feet.

Not a single flight attendant was in sight, which made me even more nervous. I looked back at the men, whispering back and forth, and the head guy gestured again for me to come join them.

Out of curiosity, I took off my seat belt and made my way down the aisle.

"*Shacharit*," the man loudly whispered.

"What the hell is going on?" I asked.

"Tefillah," the man whispered back.

One of the other two men casually grabbed my arm and held it out to the third guy, who then popped open his briefcase. I didn't know what to make of the long black leather rope with a box at the end of it that the man pulled out. He started wrapping the leather rope around my arm. After the rope was wrapped all the way up my arm, the man rested the little box in my hand securing it in place with the end of the rope; then they pulled out a second rope with a box at the end and began wrapping it around my forehead.

I grabbed the rope out of his hand. "What is this? What are you doing?"

"Tefillin," the head guy whispered as he tapped the little box. "Tefillin," which meant nothing to me. Then he pulled a similar rope out of his own briefcase and began wrapping it around his own head, then opened a Bible, pointed to a verse, and quietly hymned out a few lines to me.

This was some kind of prayer ritual. I nodded to confirm that I understood. I looked down at the duffel bag at our feet. What did they have in there? Guns? Blades? I thought about reaching into the bag myself. What the hell was I supposed I do?! I couldn't just stand there and let a terrorist plot happen. There I was, standing at the back of a plane to Israel, among three guys strapping some sort of explosive devices to all of our heads and saying their last prayers.

They finished their chant and then the head guy grabbed the duffel bag off the floor and walked out into the cabin of the plane. The other two guys put their hands on my back and nudged me to follow. I started debating with myself whether or not I thought I could take all three of them.

We got halfway up the aisle and stopped. The head guy kneeled down and reached into the bag —my heart was pounding—and the other two guys' hands were still on my back. My muscles tensed up. I was mentally preparing to tackle the guy, depending on what he pulled out of the bag.

The guy snapped around too fast for me to identify the objects in each of his hands, and he raised them straight up into the air and shouted at the top of his lungs, "*L'chaim!*"

Passenger heads started popping up to see what the commotion was, and as they turned and saw us standing in the aisle, they got excited, raised their hands, and shouted back, "*L'chaim!*"

"The fuck is going on?" I asked nobody in particular.

Then the man lowered his hands to show me the two glasses he was holding. *Is that vodka?* He extended one of the glasses to me, and when I took it, he held his up, we clinked glasses, and tossed back the vodka. A crowd assembled around us; some of the other passengers started singing prayers, and vodka bottles and shot glasses appeared out of nowhere—apparently this was the celebratory tradition for many orthodox Jews returning to Israel—as strangers clinked their glasses and repeatedly *L'chaim'd* each other as we flew into Israeli airspace, at five thirty a.m. Israel Standard Time.

In the airport, we were met by our tour guide, Guy Leibovitz, who took great pride in showing us his beautiful country, or as he put it, "*our* beautiful country." As we made our way through the city, the first thing I noticed was the plethora of machine guns dangling from shoulders all around us. The Israel Defense Forces soldiers were everywhere—walking the streets, hanging out at tourist sites, eating lunch outside of pubs with their machine guns resting on their legs—because, as they explained to us, "In Israel, you never know." We spent a lot of time hanging out with the soldiers, and one of

them, Roni, took a liking to me. As she flirted through a fellow soldier interpreter—"She wants to ask whether you have a girlfriend.
She says you're handsome. She wants to ask whether you would like
to share a shwarma pita?"—it felt so weird to think that this tiny,
gorgeous little woman could have easily kicked my ass.

We went to Golan Heights and to Jerusalem. We saw Mount
Zion; we visited the temples of Kings David and Solomon; we laid
our hands on the Western Wall; we swam in the Dead Sea; at Yad
Vashem, we spoke with a Holocaust survivor; we went to the Valley
of Elah, where David allegedly whipped Goliath's ass with a pebble;
and we saw the hill of Calvary, where Jesus supposedly died. I asked
our guide whether that had been where the crucifixion took place.
He replied, "Yes, the Romans murdered some Jews over there a long
time ago."

On our last night, we rode camels into the Negev desert, where
we spent the night under the stars. Roni cuddled herself under my
arm and began asking questions through the interpreter sitting
nearby: "What's America like? What do you do for work over there?
How did you start your own food company?" Her last question swept
me away to that Sunday when I first cooked the food in my condo
kitchen: I'd had no experience, no culinary skills, and no real direction, but I also hadn't needed anything to get going. Nothing had
stopped me from creating a company and then learning the rest as
I went. I remembered that feeling of ambition I'd had and the sense
that anything was possible. As I told Roni my story, I began to feel a
sense of passion again.

I thought about the Holocaust survivor who had lost everything—
all his physical possessions, his childhood, his freedom, and his parents
and close friends, who were murdered right in front of him—and yet
he bounced back to make something of his life. Who was I to whine
about my piddly little problems? How could *I* not think I had the
same ability to bounce back? What I was going through was nothing
compared to that!

I had lost my company. *OK, so I'll start a new one.*

I had lost all my money. *I'll sell a bunch of stuff and make it all back.*

I had lost Brie. *No, I didn't. We had four great years together, and now it's on to the next chapter.*

As we lay there in the sand, the two of us sharing my duffel bag for a pillow and staring up at the sky, I started to form a comeback plan. Upon returning home, I decided, I would dust myself off and rebuild what I had started, only this time I would do things right.

17

HOW TO START A FOOD COMPANY FROM SCRATCH WITH ZERO MONEY

I spent a week arguing with myself, trying to talk the stubborn ready-fire-aim version of myself out of getting back into the food business. I tried to convince myself to open another gym, spend a year growing it to be the best in the city, systemize it, and then start selling franchises, but what I needed was to right what I had previously wronged. I had to start from scratch and create a bigger, better, and—most important—ethical food company. Luckily, I already knew what it took to build a national wholesale food business. All I had to do was reassemble the pieces.

My plan was to call up retailers—gyms, chiropractors, physicians, grocery stores, restaurants—and get them to place preorders. Then I would turn around and use that money to buy the food, hire chefs, produce the labels, etc. But to take preorders on such a massive scale, I needed to re-create the old website.

An irritating side effect of not having any money was that I had no Wi-Fi, so in order to build this new website, I had to rely on public hot spots. Depending on the time of day, I would bounce among coffee shops, fast-food chains, hotel parking lots, and the public library.

After only three weeks of bouncing from hot spot to hot spot, and thanks to hundreds of how-to videos on YouTube and Google, I was able to assemble a fully functioning, exact-if-not-better emulation of my old thirty-thousand-dollar website for a total of nineteen dollars and ninety-nine cents. It accepted credit cards, had an integrated back-end system that engaged customers with autoresponders, automatically produced food-packing slips *with* accurate shipping labels, and sent out marketing campaigns, just like Infusionsoft.

Once I had my back-end system in place, it was time to begin selling.

Taking preorders for food that didn't yet exist was a risky maneuver. When people buy something, they don't want to wait months to get it, so if I took too long to produce the meals, and people got frustrated and began demanding refunds, I'd be fucked.

Since I was cold-calling people from public places like Starbucks and the library, when I had a phone meeting with an interested prospect, I would run out to my car, turn on the engine to block the sounds of cars driving by, people yapping, and dogs barking, and pretend to be in my office. Sometimes, for effect I'd interrupt the conversation to shout, "Yes, Emily?!—I'm sorry, [first name], can you hang on for one second?—yes, what is it Emily? No, you'll have to tell him that won't work for today. Tell him I can squeeze him in at exactly two thirty tomorrow afternoon, but that's all I've got this week . . . OK, thank you, Emily. Sorry about that, [first name]. Now, where were we?" The bigger the person's name was, the more I acted like he was interrupting my day. If I was on the phone with a known multimillionaire CEO of a giant corporation, I'd use my "I'm really busy here, but I guess I'll give you a chance to buy my product" tone, even though I was the one calling him from my car office in a McDonald's parking lot.

> CEO: OK, Mr. Philips, I've got five minutes before my
> next meeting. What d'ya got?

Me: Actually, I only have two minutes before mine, but that's all I need to show how I can quadruple your retail revenue. What are you averaging fourteen, fifteen hundred a month in retail?

CEO: Yeah, that sounds about right.

Me: Well, the facilities I work with, similar to yours, have jumped from around fifteen hundred a month to averaging five thousand eight hundred per month, *per* location—and those are the ones that don't do shit for advertising.

CEO: But we're in the health business, not the food business. I'm going to have to pass.

Me: Come on, [*In a tone you would use to guilt an old friend you haven't seen in years into skipping a work meeting and grabbing a coffee with you*] you know that the moment your staff offers nutrition advice—which they do with every damn client who walks through your door—you *are* in the food business. And here's where you're really losing money: without my ready-to-go meals on-site, your staff sends your customers across the street to your competitor— who's already selling my product—and essentially hands them *your* revenue.

CEO: Well . . . that is a good point . . . But we're not licensed to handle food.

Me: Neither is your competitor—we handle all that on my end.

CEO: OK, I suppose we *could* test it out at one location and see how it goes.

Me: Fair enough, but I'll tell you what I'd be willing to do: if you'll commit to a trial run in a minimum of ten of your locations, I'll have one of my sales guys [*whom I'd have to hire as soon as I got off the phone*] conduct an on-site tasting at each one. After one

month, you can have a look at the numbers and I
guarantee you'll be *more* than thrilled with what
you see.

CEO: [*After a brief pause*] "OK, how much of an up front
investment are we talking? [*Translated: "Whom do I
make the check out to?"*]

After two weeks of cold calls, I'd scrounged up a dozen or so gym
franchises, medical facilities, and online fitness personalities—plus, I
had started working with Sara again—who were willing to do a trial run.
Combined, they gave me access to more than one million customers.

Once the money hit the account, everything went into action:
I payed off a few back months' worth of bills so I could get back
into the kitchen space, then I called as many of the old chefs as I
could—one of whom was Li'l Mikey—and rebuilt a kitchen crew,
who helped me source food purveyors that were organic, natural,
and wholesome. We sourced only top-quality ingredients, so that we
wouldn't need to rely on any label tricks. The cooks began creating
samples for taste testing, the new nutrition facts got calculated, cooking procedures were scripted, content was created to market the new
menu, and branded labels were designed and printed.

Everyone was trained on the new machinery—particularly the
giant vacuum sealer, which the new guys loved running Li'l Mikey's
personal items through. His car keys, his lip balm, his inhaler—which
they would run through the machine four or five times in our thick-
est plastic film, then sneak it back onto his workstation. When Li'l
Mikey noticed what they'd done, at the mere sight of his entrapped
breathing device, he would naturally panic and start panting heavily.
But the funniest was when they would quadruple-seal Li'l Mikey's
cell phone and then call it from a blocked number, so that they could
watch him panic as he struggled to rip through the numerous plastic
layers, only to have the phone hang up as soon as he got to it. "Oh,
real funny, guys!" he would whine, still not realizing they were the

ones calling. "What if that was my doctor, or my kid's school, or something!" to which the other guys would cackle their asses off.

As I worked vigorously on my new mission, I no longer needed alcohol as an emotional Novocain. I felt free again. I was excited. I was energized. Stress was nothing more than a buzzing fly that got flicked away with each new microproject I undertook to get my new company up and running. It wasn't until after the sun went down each day that I would join the chefs for a social drink, and even then I didn't feel that I *needed* a drink. Instead of an entire liter of vodka at night, I had a few Red Bull vodkas—not to calm my nerves, but to enjoy myself.

After a few months of around-the-clock team effort and an entire crew with matching purple bags under their eyes, my food machine was up and running at full speed again. Once all the new meals were prepared, I stood in the minus-ten-degree freezer room all day making sure every little detail was perfect. There was no room for error on this initial run: Was each food package visually beautiful? Were the grill marks on each salmon dish perfectly crisscrossed? Was each slice of steak identically as pink as the one beside it? If one dish had an inconsistency, it was tossed and a new one was made.

Had every single meal been cooked, chilled, and frozen at the exact right time and temperature to ensure safety and quality? *If not, toss and redo.* Did the shipping labels match the packing slips, and did both match the privately labeled packaging? We couldn't have a vegan weight-loss center opening up a package of steak and chicken meals, or a bodybuilding gym opening up a package of meals labeled "CrossFit Meals"—that wouldn't have gone over well. I barely noticed that my fingers were numb or that my nose was runny as I bounced around the freezer room checking, documenting, *re*checking, taking pictures, then *triple*-checking every element of every food package to be shipped.

I was counting the number of meals in each cooler and comparing their packing slips when I heard Li'l Mikey yelling behind me,

"Come on guys! This shit's not funny anymore!" Then he noticed me against the back wall. "Oh, hey, Jeff! Do you think you could give me a hand?"

"Hey, guys," I said to the culprits on the other side of the locked freezer door, "let him go." The door opened. Li'l Mikey thanked me profusely and then sprinted back to the production room, cursing at his captors.

Once I felt confident that everything was perfect, I stood back and stared at the meals for a minute, taking in all that was sitting in front of me: new company, new crew, new customers, new website, new meals, new packaging. And then, after all the early mornings leaching Wi-Fi outside the Holiday Inn, the late nights in the kitchen collaborating with the chefs, all the stress and depression, the excitement and anticipation, I finally had something tangible—something to be proud of—sitting in front of me.

One week after the meals were shipped, feedback started coming in: every single customer had absolutely fallen in love with the food, *and*—the best news of all—customers were once again losing seven pounds in seven days!

18

THE CEO'S DILEMMA: TO SELL OR NOT TO SELL (SHITTY FOOD)

I'd forgotten how sexy Sara was until I saw her walk through the front door—her muscular olive legs ripping through the bottom of her tiny black dress. The hostess pointed in my direction, and as soon as Sara spotted me, she ran over to give me a giant hug and buried her face into my chest. As soon as we sat down, she immediately started fiddling under the table.

"I'm not going to stop you from doing anything you want," I told her, "but you might want to save that for after we leave."

"*Ooooh*, you're right," she moaned. We ordered two Long Islands. I'd burnt out my vodka Red Bull tooth.

The server returned two minutes later holding two tall, skinny glasses with black straws.

"Wow! That's a good Long Island," Sara said. "This could be trouble for me, *mi amigo*."

"Yeah," I confirmed, "A few of these can even get to *me*!"

"Hey, that reminds me: you're not supposed to be driving any-way, are you?"

"Nah, I took care of that."

"*Lo manejó?* What do you mean, you took care of it?"

"Oh, no big deal."

"Tell me!" She clung to my arm and whined like an eigh-year-old begging to go to the candy store. "I want to know!"

"OK, but you can't tell anybody."

She pretended to pull a zipper over her lips. "*Sellados.*"

"So there's this military recruiter at my gym—cool guy, a little older than I am—and he wouldn't shut up about the benefits of being in the army. So I was just being friendly and asked him, 'Oh, yeah? But what's the age cutoff?' He said, 'Thirty-five. How old are you?' 'Just turned thirty,' I told him, and he got all animated, 'You're plenty young! And you'd be perfect: the physical part would be a cakewalk for you, and you seem like you've got a good head on your shoul-ders.' Then he asked whether I had a clean record, and so I told him about the DUI. 'Is that the only thing on your record?' he asked, to which I replied yes. 'Oh, that's nothing. Give me your information; I'll take care of that, and then we'll get you signed up.'"

"So you're going into the army now?" Sara sarcastically asked.

"No, they'd kick my smart-ass out the first day."

"So . . ."

"So he *did* wipe my record clean—I don't know how he did it; I didn't ask—but what was done was done and then I just told him I had changed my mind."

"Was he pissed?"

"A little, at first, just because I cost him his monthly quota, and he got bitched out by his superior. Other than that, he was fine."

"So your record is clean now, just like that?"

"Yep! I'm sure it still shows up on there *somewhere*, but for all general purposes, I'm good to go."

"That could only happen to you, *chulo*." Then she leaned in for another peck on the lips.

"So what did you have in mind?"

"I'm not sure. This seared cod sounds good."

"No, *smart-ass*, what did you have in mind for the business agreement?"

"Well, I'd be good with the same agreement we had last time—"

"You couldn't keep up your half of the bargain last time," she cut me off. "*Buuut*, I kind of like having you indebted to me. *Muy, muy en deuda conmigo.*"

"I like it too—for two reasons! The obvious one and the money one."

"*Sí!*" she agreed. "So how's the new food?"

"You'll love it; it's even better than before. I've got some for you to take back with you so your clients can get a little tease, and then, if you take a preorder from them, they'll essentially pay for your full inventory and then some."

"*Sí*, I can do a tasting when I get back. I've already thought about it. If I set the regular retail price at seven fifty per meal, then I'll have an ongoing special 'buy four, get one free,' which will bring their price down to six per meal. Nobody will ever buy fewer than five at a time."

I looked up and saw the hostess coming around the corner. My stomach dropped and I felt all the blood leave my face.

"What is it, baby?" Sara turned to see what had spooked me so badly. "Is everything OK?"

My mouth was open but I couldn't speak. All I could do was stare.

The hostess turned and started heading my way, and following closely behind her was the Extortion Cougar, all dolled up and accompanied by her husband and two children. *Two children!*

"Who is that, babe?" Sara asked, but I couldn't talk.

When she noticed me, she froze like a deer in headlights. This was the first time I'd seen her with even a hint of vulnerability. *I* now had the leverage to flip *her* life upside down—and we both knew it.

As the Cougar's family approached my table, she nervously raised her eyebrows and tilted her head to the side, to personify a very subtle *truce* with a question mark at the end. All I could think about was what she'd done to my wheels. I wanted to go up and humiliate her in front of her husband. But I just gave her a slight nod with my eyes closed to confirm the unspoken peace treaty. At that, she broke eye contact and brushed coldly by my table, following the hostess to a different part of the restaurant. Then our food came, and over dinner I told Sara the whole story.

As we were walking across the parking lot, I heard someone from the back alley of the restaurant shout in my direction, "You lucked out tonight, Philips!"

"Oh, yeah?" I turned to see who the trash-talker was, but all I could make out was a short figure standing behind a metal fence. "Why's that?"

"Because if I had known you were in there earlier," the shadowy figure fired back, "I would have fucked with your food."

I walked around the fence to the opening on the far side and found Chef Kevin on a cigarette break.

"I didn't know you were working here. How's it going?"

"How the fuck do you think it's going? I'm working in another shit hole, with a group of fucktards dumber than the last one—if that's even possible." I couldn't help laughing. "But life could be worse," he half smiled. "I could still be working for you."

"Still the same chipper SOB as always," I said as I slapped him on the shoulder. "Sara, this is Chef Kevin; he designed all the original meals your clients used to love."

"Oh, the famous Chef Kevin," she said in a way that made him sound legendary. "Your chicken curry sauce was my *faaavorite!*"

"This asshole," he said as he pointed to me, "desperately needed my help. His food was shit before that."

"I thought you'd have been running a restaurant downtown by now," I said to him. "That or murdered by your own kitchen crew."

"The dickheads at those places want me to work too many hours, and they say I've gotta be 'nice to my coworkers' . . . fuck that!" He took a long puff of his cigarette. "This place doesn't give a shit."

The back door of the restaurant slammed open and a young man in a polo shirt tucked into his creased khakis stepped out and shouted, "Kevin! Smoke break's over. We need you back at your station."

Without even turning his head, Kevin dryly responded, "Fuck off, Tim," and the young man chuckled, then ducked his head back inside.

"I thought of you the other day," Kevin said to me.

"Oh, yeah? What was I wearing?" I asked.

"Fuck you," he said as he took another long puff of his cigarette. "Ya know, those Nutrisystem assholes call me every week trying to sell me food—I don't even know how they got my fucking number. A couple of weeks ago, I finally bought a few meals just to get 'em off my ass, and they *still* keep calling! What an annoying bunch of shitheads. They reminded me of you."

I'd been teaching my new guys how sales scripts work, and I would have them gather around while I called Nutrisystem, offering a new problem so my guys could see how the Nutrisystem employee overcame it. I would *really* lead the Nutrisystem rep into selling me a ton of food, then, right before I finished giving him the last four digits of a phony credit card number, a fake emergency arose, and I would give them my number so they could follow up with me later

"My cell phone? Sure, it's [Chef Kevin's real number], and let me give you my email too, just in case, it's [Chef Kevin's real email], and *please* be sure to follow up with me."

That grumpy bastard had no clue why he was getting weekly calls and follow-up emails from what must have been, by then, at least a dozen different Nutrisystem reps, and it made me smile to think of Cryin' Kevin viciously laying into the poor, commission-seeking sales reps who were just following up as requested.

"Well, man," I said as Kevin finished his cigarette, "I'll let you get back in there."

I shook his hand, and then Kevin walked back inside the restaurant, somehow managing to exude anger and contentedness at the same time.

—

"I can't believe you chose this place."

"Oh, are you kidding?" Manny said in his strong Swedish accent. "They've got the best brick-oven pizza in town!"

"That's my point. We're not going to go two seconds without someone coming up to our table."

"So tell me: how were sales this week? Did you guys kill it with those new meals?"

"Actually, that's why I invited you here," he said his tone becoming more serious. "I've kind of got bad news—"

"Well, lookie, lookie," a woman shouted in our direction, "Whom do we have here? Manny and Jeff Scot, eating pizza and drinking beer."

"Betsy!" I turned around and gave her a hug.

"I knew you guys weren't as healthy as you claimed."

"Betsy, did you not learn anything in my seminars?" I asked. "This is a meat lover's pizza, and, of course, beer has hops, which is a vegetable, so we're just getting our veggies and protein in."

"Yeah, yeah, whatever you say. It was good to see you two, but I've gotta run. Ciao!"

"Good call on picking this place," I said as I rolled my eyes. "So, anyway, you were saying . . ."

"Well, the gym members hardly bought any of the new food last week. The first few weeks they were all caught up in the excitement, but now they're saying it's too expensive."

"Too expensive?" I snapped. "This is genuinely organic, wholesome food—it's supposed to be more expensive."

"I know," Manny agreed. "I'm just telling you what they're saying."

"So you've still got your entire inventory?"

"Unfortunately, yeah. So I won't be placing an order this week."

But it wasn't just Manny; the next day Sara, of all people, called to tell me she wouldn't be placing an order, either. Then one of my franchise accounts said none of their fifty-plus locations needed to place an order, and then my second-biggest online affiliate, an up-and-coming fitness guru out of Texas, said none of her 250,000 clients were placing any orders that week. Next, I got a call from a grocery chain, telling me that my product was being bumped next month for a product that was moving off the shelves better. *All* of my retailers were relaying the exact same feedback. "Our customers love the food, they love the results, but it's just too expensive." I hung up on a gym owner in Colorado when he suggested, "You should use cheaper ingredients so you can drop your meals down to Nutrisystem prices."

This wasn't a mystery to me. Of course, if customers have two choices in front of them—a highly priced one and a cheaply priced one—and both labels claim to have equally healthy ingredients, most people are going to go for the cheaper one. They had no way of knowing that my competitors were lying to them; only I knew that.

Determined to stand my ground this time, I came up with an interim solution: I chopped the menu down to only a handful of options and then aggregately pooled *all* the customer orders from all of my different retailers so that I could order a bulk amount of fewer items, in turn dropping my price. On top of that, I dropped my margins down to next to nothing in order to bring the consumer price to a more palatable level.

This was a successful band-aid for the issue on the consumers' side, but it created an unsuspected issue on the purveyor's side: the organic suppliers couldn't consistently provide the quantities I needed. I was caught in a frustrating supply-demand pickle; the healthy food cost too much, but the cheaper food was unacceptable to my customers.

When I couldn't give my retailers and their customers what they wanted, they began selling for my competitors—Big-brand "organic" companies, some of which had been publically busted by the FDA for using nonorganic ingredients. They were doing exactly what I had done before—lying about the quality of their food. When consumers bought food that they *thought* was healthy, they were bumping genuinely healthy food off of the shelves, and so, ironically, the more they tried to eat healthy, the harder it was to find healthy foods—in this case, my foods.

I'd thought that without financial puppet masters I would be able to do the right thing, but as it turned out, investors were only one of many inhibiting factors in the food industry equation. The unfortunate reality I was learning about the food and weight-loss industries was that Adam Smith's invisible hand was directly forcing corruption.

Corruption creeps in when the market starts demanding something that nobody's got—salty and sweet food that's low in salt and sugar—and one of my ballsy, or perhaps shrewd, competitors uses the food label loopholes to claim it had it anyway. What you ended up with was cheap, tasty shit with some fancy-shmancy label narrative alleging just how nutritious the piece of shit was.

Under the pressure of lying competitors, duped consumers, and indifferent retailers, and at the immediate risk of, once again, going out of business, I decided to play the game again. One at a time, I reinstated all the little label tactics I had learned. The discrete ingredients tactic, the portion size tactic, the dwindling serving size tactic, the distribution tactic, the label padding tactic, the masking tactic, the fat-free, sugar-free, gluten-free tactic, the ingredients claims tactic, the "cleaning up the ingredients" tactic. And last but not least, the distraction tactic, in which I use terms like "free-range," "cage-free" and "humanely raised" to take your mind off the fact you were eating crappy food. Whenever I'm in the grocery store, it still drives me nuts when I see people paying extra money for free-range, grass-fed hot dogs—*fucking hot dogs, people!*

My customers came roaring back.

I was then reaching more people than ever before; I was making more money than ever before; and even though these people were going to keep gaining weight and wonder why, I was hearing better feedback from customers than ever before.

I knew what I needed to do.

19

GLUTEN-FREE WAS A SCAM: CONFESSIONS OF A RECOVERING HEALTH-FOOD HUSTLER

"One more trip ought to do it," I said to Dave as I held the kitchen door open for him.

"What else can I help carry to your car?" he asked.

I grabbed a stack of cooking trays and handed it to him. "Do you remember the time Babs had, like, eight of these trays full of sweet potato fries but forgot to set the oven timers and ruined all of them, and then when I tried to eat one—to stop her from crying—I shattered my back tooth to pieces?"

"How could I forget?! I walked in and you were spitting blood into a trash can, Babs was wailing in the corner, and the place was so smoky we had to clear out for, like, an hour."

We laughed together. It seemed like every piece of equipment we touched had a great story attached to it. I glanced into the office to make sure I hadn't forgotten anything and then pulled the door shut.

"Remember the time we were all crammed in there, hiding from the health inspector, and Vic got light-headed, and started spinning in circles?"

Both of us let out a long, wheezing laugh, and then Dave finished the story in a red-faced squeal. "And then that poor bastard passed out, leaning over the freezer, and then Donavon—" *Wheeeze!* "Donavon pulled out a Sharpie and drew all over his face!"

We were struggling to breathe over our own laughter.

"Feels like it was yesterday!" I said as I caught my breath.

"So, if you don't mind me asking, what made you decide to sell the biz?"

"Well, to be honest with you—"

I felt my phone buzzing in my pocket, and when I pulled it out, I couldn't believe the name I saw on the screen: "Hurricane Babs."

"Dave, I'm going to grab this call really quick," I told him. "I'll meet you in the parking lot in just a minute."

I pressed my Bluetooth, "Hey, stranger! How are you?"

"Oh, I'm doing fine," Babs said in the slowest, calmest voice I'd ever heard. "I just wanted to call you and apologize for the way I was and the things I used to put you through, and I really hope you can forgive me."

I assured her, "Babs, no need to apologize; it's all in the past. I'm just glad you're doing good!"

She began whining, "Jeff, I *really* need you to say you forgive me." She started crying and sniffling. "I need to hear the words, pleeeaaase."

I could see the image of her pouty face. "Babs, please don't cry. Of course I forgive you—I was honestly never upset with you."

"Thank you." *Sniffle.* "It means a lot to me, and I just want you to know I really liked working with you and everything you did for me."

"I enjoyed working with you too. Where are you now?"

"Chip got me a job selling real estate."

"Oh, wow. So no more food for you, then? I guess that means no more cuts or burns!"

"Oh, no. They have a Babs chart here too. Last week, while I was showing this young couple how the glass-top stove in their new home worked, I leaned on the wrong spot and burned myself."

"Well, I'm glad to know you're still yourself." We both laughed.

Before hanging up, she told me that Casey was working in some Cajun eatery in downtown Roanoke (just to be safe, I've made it a point ever since to never visit any of the restaurants in the proximity) and in his spare time was—ironically and inexplicably—an Uber driver.

In the parking lot, Dave was cramming the giant stack of cooking trays into my car.

"You'll never guess who that was—Hurricane Babs, apologizing for her explosion."

"Really?" Dave asked in disbelief.

"Even crazier: I forgot to tell you, I got a call from Aaron the other week . . ." Dave's eyes widened. "He left FCG!"

"Get the hell out of here!"

"Apparently he couldn't handle Jason's BS anymore. He said that *everyone* has left because of him."

"Hmm . . . I guess we all needed a fresh start," Dave confirmed. "Which reminds me: why are *you* selling the biz?"

"Oh, right, why I'm hanging it up. Well, to be honest, I hate what I do every day. I lie. All day, every day, for the past year and a half, since starting fresh again, I've told fucking lies. I tell people that gluten and GMOs are the devil, I create marketing material with buzzwords I can't stand, like calories and metabolism. I put stickers on my food that say nonsense things like paleo and all-natural—rhetoric that doesn't mean a goddamn thing, and yet it consumes my life. I can't take this shit anymore."

"Why don't you just stop doing the stuff you hate?"

"I am. If you don't talk about that kind of crap, then people won't buy food from you, so . . . I'm not selling anymore."

"So, then, do you think the food industry is fucked?"

"No, not completely fucked. It's fixable."

"Fixable how?"

"Well, off the top, a lateral franchise farming system would level the playing field for government subsidies. A day-trading firm that bundles *genuinely* organic commodities into things like exchange-traded funds would help bridge the price gap between organics and nonorganics. Of course, getting money out of politics by reversing Citizens United would chop down Monsanto's lobbying power, and then—"

"Whoa, man . . . I have no idea what the fuck you just said."

"Yeah," I chuckled. "I know. I'm just glad you picked up when I called."

"I'm not going to lie. I was pretty pissed at you for a while. But once I heard about what Jason did to you, I realized it wasn't your fault."

"I'm just glad you're back," I said before giving him a handshake hug. "Now we can move on to our next venture."

"We did the fitness thing. We did the food thing. What do you have in mind next?"

I didn't even have to think about it. "I'll tell you what we're going to do: spread the message."

"We're going to start with an experiment," I said to the sea of people sitting below the stage looking up at me. "Your best friend has just returned from the doctor and he has just been diagnosed with type 2 diabetes *and* is at serious risk of a heart attack. Now your friend doesn't know a thing about nutrition, so he's relying on you to help him make smarter choices. So you're going to help him pick out his breakfast by looking at a few different food labels."

I pressed the clicker and the projector switched on.

Nutrition Facts	
Serving Size 1	
Servings Per Container	
Amount Per Serving	
Calories 89	Calories from Fat
	% Daily Value*
Total Fat 0g	
Total Carbohydrate 3.2g	
Protein 1g	
*Percent Daily Values are based on a 2,000 calorie diet.	

Nutrition Facts	
Serving Size 1	
Servings Per Container	
Amount Per Serving	
Calories 95	Calories from Fat
	% Daily Value*
Total Fat .3g	
Total Carbohydrate 25g	
Protein .5g	
*Percent Daily Values are based on a 2,000 calorie diet.	

"Not a huge difference between these two, but one number should jump out at you, and your friend's life hangs in the balance here, so we've got to make the best choice possible. May I see a show of hands if you would pick the one on the right for your friend?"

Zero hands went up.

"OK, then, just to make sure my mic is working, may I see a show of hands if you would pick the one on the left for your friend to eat for breakfast?"

Every hand went up.

"All right, well let's see what you would have chosen for your deathly ill friend to consume."

I pressed the clicker.

Nutrition Facts
Serving Size 1
Servings Per Container

Amount Per Serving

Calories 89   Calories from Fat

% Daily Value*

Total Fat 0g

Total Carbohydrate 3.2g

Protein 1g

*Percent Daily Values are based on a 2,000 calorie diet.

Nutrition Facts
Serving Size 1
Servings Per Container

Amount Per Serving

Calories 95   Calories from Fat

% Daily Value*

Total Fat .3g

Total Carbohydrate 25g

Protein .5g

*Percent Daily Values are based on a 2,000 calorie diet.

"Now, I could put up a good argument as to why the one on the left might be the better choice," I said as the audience laughed, "but let's take the fun out and give your friend one more option."

I changed the slide again.

Nutrition Facts
Serving Size 1
Servings Per Container

Amount Per Serving

Calories 50   Calories from Fat

% Daily Value*

Total Fat 2g

Total Carbohydrate 0g

Protein 3g

*Percent Daily Values are based on a 2,000 calorie diet.

Nutrition Facts
Serving Size 1
Servings Per Container

Amount Per Serving

Calories 105   Calories from Fat

% Daily Value*

Total Fat .4g

Total Carbohydrate 27g

Protein 1.3g

*Percent Daily Values are based on a 2,000 calorie diet.

"Now, keep in mind your friend is a diabetic, so excess sugar, aka carbohydrates, can be very harmful to him."

When I asked to see hands, the audience once again uniformly agreed on the one on the left.

"Well, let's see what you've chosen for your friend to eat for breakfast this morning," I said, and pressed the clicker.

Nutrition Facts
Serving Size 1
Servings Per Container

Amount Per Serving

Calories 50   Calories from Fat

% Daily Value*

Total Fat 2g

Total Carbohydrate 0g

Protein 3g

*Percent Daily Values are based on a 2,000 calorie diet.

Nutrition Facts
Serving Size 1
Servings Per Container

Amount Per Serving

Calories 105   Calories from Fat

% Daily Value*

Total Fat .4g

Total Carbohydrate 27g

Protein 1.3g

*Percent Daily Values are based on a 2,000 calorie diet.

"Y'all are some shitty friends," I joked as the room roared with laughter. "I hope I don't ever need your help picking out *my* breakfast.

"But, to be fair to you, judging by the label alone, yes, dog shit would be healthier than a banana for a diabetic to eat, but, obviously, if you take away the labels, then choosing breakfast for your sick friend becomes a no-brainer."

I pressed the clicker one last time.

They erupted into laughter again, and I had successfully primed the audience.

"As you all probably know, I had a food company, and yes, *I* used to manipulate my labels. I didn't do it to trick people into eating dog shit. I did it because when consumers—you, I, we—pay attention to a food label, we stop paying attention to the food it represents.

"You see, without a food label to fixate on, it becomes self-evident that sugary cereals, bars of synthesized food, chips, beer, and dog shit *aren't* good choices for people who are trying to lose weight! The problem is, as long as food labels remain there and you think that reading them gives you information about your food, companies can—and will—maneuver, manipulate, morph, hype, promote, polarize, and all-around bullshit their food labels, and what you think you know about them, to get you to buy more food.

"The only way you guys can be tricked into having a debate about which coconut water is better for you—Harmless Harvest, Vita Coco, Juice Press, Taste Nirvana, or Zico—is if you're paying attention to the label instead of seeing the drink for what it really is. These brands wouldn't be able to sell you a bottle of low-calorie, coconut-flavored sugar water if you weren't preemptively conditioned by the health industry to (a) believe that excessive calories are bad, (b) think that coconut is healthy, and (c) check the label for these types of things. If you're not diligently scanning the label, then they can't distract you from the fact that you're just drinking pure sugar.

"The cold truth is, food labels *aren't* there to educate you; they're there to help us market to you.

"You see, food packages are like little books: they're there to tell you a story about what's in the package, but since they're written by the person trying to sell it—my competitors and I—they come with a bias. The women in the audience can relate to this," I said as I lightened my inflections to a jokey tone. "Any and all verbiage on a box or wrapper of food is like anything that comes out of a guy's mouth pre-intercourse: it's manipulative, it's exaggerated, and its sole purpose is aimed at closing the sale." The women nodded their heads in agreement as they looked at each other and laughed.

"As you know, some of the hottest nutrition buzzwords at the moment are paleo, gluten-free, grass-fed, organic, no added sugar, omega 3s, and antioxidants. Now, take a look at this paleo, *gluten*-free, grass-fed, organic protein bar that has no added sugar and is packed with omega 3s and antioxidants." I pressed the clicker to reveal a brand-name protein bar, touting these claims all over its label.

"How many of you have eaten one of these bars before?"

Roughly half the hands in the room went up.

"Well, let me ask you a question: do you think this bar *really* has pure, organic lamb meat in it—show of hands?"

All the same hands went up.

"Ha!" I said playfully. "So if this bar of ingredients—which was assembled in one of General Mills's industrial warehouses—is so pure, then how come that grass-fed, organic lamb meat doesn't spoil after sitting on a room-temperature shelf for six months?"

The mumble of the crowd was a good indicator that that fact had never crossed their minds before.

"Question number two: how many of you are familiar with the term 'omega 3'?"

The majority of the hands went up.

"Excellent. And can anyone tell me what an omega 3 is?"

The hands quickly fell back to their laps.

"Omega 3 is a fancy word for fat. Now think about the simple psychology at work here: if the label said, '*added fat*,' you would shy away from it, wouldn't you? But by changing the word to an important-sounding term you vaguely recognize, you now see it as a healthy bonus to this food bar.

"How about antioxidants; anybody heard of that term before?"

Everyone raised their hand.

"And does anybody know what those are, or why they're supposed to be healthy for you?"

No volunteers.

"So then let me ask you a very *caaalm*, *seeensible* question: Why the fuck are you seeking them out, then?!" The room erupted in laughter.

A hand in the middle of the room shot up. "But aren't foods high in omega 3s and antioxidants good for you?"

"That completely depends on the food that contains those things. Getting omega 3's by eating salmon is good for you; getting them from a bar of food that has more sugar than a Pixy Stix, probably not. All plants contain antioxidants, but while getting them from eating broccoli is good for you, getting them from cocaine—which comes from the coca plant—probably isn't. Do you see how this works? As long as you're distracted by the microelements of food, to the point of reading food labels to seek them out, I can trick you into buying pretty much any shitty product I want to push, because you're focusing on the wrong things.

"If you're trying to lose weight, then you shouldn't be eating a ton of cookies, and you already know this, right? But if I'm a cookie company, and I know that you think protein is good and GMOs are bad, for example, all I have to do is market a protein cookie that doesn't have GMOs, and now I've got you eating cookies again, which is completely counterproductive to your weight loss.

"But this isn't your fault. I'll tell you why you think these things are healthy for you: it's because we've trained you to think that. As a food manufacturer, and especially as a supplement wholesaler and retailer, I've learned the value of highlighting individual macro- and microingredients so that I can sell you on their health benefits. It's the best way to get label readers to buy something they likely wouldn't buy otherwise.

"And here's something you didn't know about yourself. . . . May I please have two volunteers?"

An eager woman tapped her friend on the arm and pressured her to join her onstage. "The thing that you don't know about yourself, but that you're all victims of, is that just by seeing buzzwords like gluten-free on a food package, for example, you're 33 percent more likely to buy it. Or put another way, you're 33 percent less likely to make the smartest available choice. Now, statistics are boring as hell. I like visual examples better." I pulled a blindfold from my pocket and asked the two women which of them wanted to be the blind grocery shopper. The eager woman volunteered her friend to do the honor, so I tied the handkerchief over her eyes and pulled some random food items out of my bag—half of them were boxed goods and the other half were random fruits and veggies—and distributed them evenly on each of the two tables beside me.

"These tables represent two aisles in the grocery store. I'll let you," I said as I pointed to the eager woman, "go shopping down this aisle. And I'll let you," I said as I grabbed the blindfolded woman's arm and guided her to the other table, "do your shopping on this aisle. There are ten items on each of your tables, but you're only going to buy three of them, so your goal is to pick the three healthiest items," I said and handed them each a cloth grocery bag. "On your mark, get set, *go!*"

It was immediately evident who was going to win. The woman without the blindfold picked up each item and began examining it closely. She was trying to figure out which ones had the most vitamins, or the fewest calories, or whatever the hell she'd been programmed to search for, while the blindfolded woman moved much more quickly. As soon as she touched an item that was in a box, since she obviously had no clue of what it was—*is this whole-grain, low-calorie Fiber One cereal or is it Pillsbury's Funfetti cake mix?*—she moved on to the items she could see with her hands. The whole potato, the apple, and the bag of grapes were an easy decision for her.

When they finished, I quizzed the nonblindfolded woman on her choices.

"Well," she said, "I chose these granola bars over the blueberries because the label said they had blueberries in them, plus a lot of other stuff."

"OK, and why the Betty Crocker mashed potatoes" I asked, "instead of this whole potato?"

"Because these are gluten-free," she said as she pointed to the wording on the box, "and it says they're 100 percent real potatoes right here, so I figured, what's the difference?"

"Interesting logic," I playfully teased her, "but fair enough. And how do you explain the brownie mix?"

"Because, look," she said as she showed me the box, "it has almonds—same as if I had chosen those mixed nuts—*and* it's made with all-natural, organic ingredients!"

I wasn't sure of whether the audience was laughing at her silly method of choosing health food or at the tilted-head, curious face I was making at her.

"All right," I said. "Well, let's see what your friend chose." I dumped the other bag back onto the table, and the label-reading woman immediately started defending herself.

"Yeah, but see: the granola bars have all the vitamins and fiber that the apple has, and mine have blueberries, which are better for you than grapes. And *my* mashed potatoes are gluten-free!"

"What if I told you, Ms. Gluten-Free Organic, that every item on both of these tables is gluten-free, all-natural, and organic. The only real difference was that half of it was real food and the other half was sugar-loaded, processing-plant food.

"You see," I said as I turned to the audience, "even if a food is genuinely gluten-free or all-natural, if you're busy reading the packaging, you don't pay attention to what's *not* on the label. In order to polarize your purchasing behavior, the label has to tell you a story in big bold print that says, 'There's no fucking gluten in me!'

"So, as you all just witnessed," I said as I laid my hands on the items the blindfolded woman picked out, "you have a 33 percent better chance of making smart, healthy choices if you go shopping blindfolded, because it *blinds* you to the industry's food-label bullshit. Fact: People on gluten-free diets are 82 percent more likely to gain weight. And why?" I waved my hand over the items that the non-blindfolded woman had chosen. "You just saw why!"

A hand shot up from the middle of the audience.

"Yes?" I said as I pointed to the hand.

"So can you tell us exactly what we should be eating?"

Each week I get a call from my sister's mother-in-law, Ruth, asking me for weight-loss advice. Ruth looks like Marisa Tomei, and she's one of the loveliest, sweetest people I've ever met. That being said, she reads every health-related blog or article she comes across and then FaceTimes me—never a phone call—to get my opinion on what they said. She'll happily listen to what I say, nodding along, taking notes, but as soon as she hangs up the iPad, she forgets everything I've told her, then dives back into her health blogs so she can jot down the same *exact* questions to ask me again the following week.

One recent week's video chat went like this:

"Hey, Jeff, such-and-such article said that it's important to calculate your macronutrients, and I just want to make sure I'm doing it right. Can you give Gerald and me your take on it?"

I dragged my hand down my face as I mentally braced myself to repeat the nutrition course I had by then conducted three weeks in a row. "Yeah, OK . . . let's do this: grab Gerald and a piece of paper."

"Gerald!" she screamed into the other room. "Come in here. Jeff's going to tell us what to do!" and then Gerald appeared in front of the camera and sat beside Ruth with an apologetic look on his face.

"Jeff, I tried to tell her not to call you with this crap again."

I waved it off as no big deal, and Ruth dove into the questions.

"OK, so how do I know how much I should be eating? What was that equation you showed me?"

"It's your ideal body weight multiplied by 0.75; so that's 120 times 0.75 equals 90 grams of protein each day, then divide it by the number of meals you eat."

"Jeff, that's too much to try to figure out each meal, can you just tell me exactly what I need to eat?"

"*Ruthieee . . .*" Gerald said in a tone you'd use to warn a child that he's about to be put in time-out.

"OK, I'll write it down," she sulked. "So what do I eat, though? What are the right proteins?"

"Write this down and laminate it, please: eggs, chicken breast, turkey—not the processed stuff from the deli—beef, lamb, pork. Y'all are lazy Jews like I am, right? You eat pork, don't you?"

Gerald leaned back so Ruth couldn't see him and tapped his chest emphatically while mouthing "I do, I do!"

"And steak, plenty and plenty of steak."

"Steak? No, I saw a news segment that said steak has too much saturated fat in it—the kind that sticks around the midsection."

Gerald rolled his eyes.

I lifted up my shirt so they could see my abs. "Please tell me more. What else did your TV nutrition guru say I should avoid eating?"

"Put steak on the list, dear," Gerald said as he smiled.

"But what if the steak has GMOs?"

I threw up my hands. "Who the hell knows, Ruth? Look, whatever invisible harm the big bad GMOs might or might not be causing, what does that have to do with your belly fat?"

Gerald tapped on the paper, signaling her to write steak on the list.

"What about seafood? What kinds are OK to eat?"

"All seafood: tilapia, shrimp, crab, salmon—"

"How many calories are in salmon?" She said as she cut me off. "This one magazine article I read says it's got a lot of calories."

"It's salmon, Ruth. You don't *need* to know how many calories are in it!"

"I really think I should count the calories. It couldn't hurt to know how many—"

"Ruth!" Gerald said as he raised his voice to make her move on.

"All right, well, what other kinds?"

I sighed. "Any seafood you want . . . mussels, swordfish, cod, tuna . . ."

"Oh, no. I read that tuna causes mercury poisoning."

I grabbed a wineglass off the counter and filled it. "You're driving me to drink early today, Ruth," I told her. Gerald pulled his own glass full of red into camera view and gave me an air cheers, then I answered her question with another question: "Ruth, do you know anybody who's ever gotten mercury poisoning?" She shook her head.

Part of the reason I was so annoyed as I sat there, listening to her misguided questions, was that I, of course, knew where all these little rumors were coming from. "Tuna causes mercury poisoning." "Meat causes cancer." "Egg yolks increase cholesterol." "Broccoli gives you diarrhea." Food companies—mine included—use these little scare tactics to convince people like Ruth to stop eating our competitors' products, among other reasons. If I'm being outsold by a tuna company then, yeah, it's in my best interest to help spread the message, for example, that tuna causes mercury poisoning, because it makes people think twice about that sweet-and-sour StarKist pouch they're about to purchase instead of my chicken meal. So, rather than addressing her specific question, I attempted to paint the broader picture for her.

"Where do you think these articles get their material from, Ruth? Food companies," I said as I tapped my finger against my chest, "are the ones creating the messages that these media sources are telling you!" If these messages weren't coming from us the media would probably be telling you: "Lean Cuisine raises blood pressure." "Pepsi causes cancer." "Kraft Macaroni & Cheese increases cholesterol." "Elisabeth Hasselbeck leads to mental deterioration." "Nutrisystem gives you diarrhea." Gerald began chuckling wildly. I took a sip of wine. "Just eat your mercury-loaded tuna and your GMO-loaded steak and you'll be fine!"

"But what if I get too muscular eating all that protein?"

I began massaging my forehead.

It's for this very reason that I tend to avoid giving individual weight-loss advice to people anymore, because—who are we kidding?—nobody uses it. Ruth doesn't, paying customers rarely do, and now, getting back to my speech, I knew damn well that the audience sitting in front of me wouldn't, either. They just wouldn't. But toward the end of a presentation that exposed how food companies like mine contributed to the audience members' poor health in the past, I felt obligated to *at least* do for them what I did for Ruth. After staring out into the sea of faces for a minute, contemplating how I could best educate them without lecturing, I decided I would let them learn vicariously.

"Tell you what," I responded to the audience member with her hand up. "I'm going to tell you what I do, and you can do whatever you want it with it."

"I personally look at my food from a bird's-eye view: protein, vegetable, starch. The second I start focusing on some minuscule microelement of my food—mercury levels, calories, GMOs—I know I'm distracted, which means I'm fucked.

"I personally don't read food labels. The things I eat don't typically have them, to begin with. When was the last time you saw a steak with a nutrition facts label? But if I'm buying oatmeal or eggs, for example, I pretend the labels aren't there. I'm guaranteed to make a smarter decision this way, because I'm not diverted into some tangential narrative about my oatmeal and eggs.

"Next—and you vegetarians in the audience may want to ear-muff it—I personally only eat proteins that had a mother. And the fewer legs, the better: cows have four, chickens have two, and fish and eggs have none—centipedes are obviously out. You'll never see me eating a bar of food, not because I'm holier than thou, but because I know that my body doesn't use it the same as animal protein. It just doesn't help my physique and health.

"I personally eat vegetables—usually green ones—twice a day, lunch and dinner. *But* I don't limit myself to only two servings, because I know I can't have too many veggies. If someone's offering me an omelet with spinach and feta, there's no chance I'm turning that down.

"I personally eat starches—brown rice, oatmeal, quinoa—same as my veggies.

"I personally eat according to math: I enjoy weighing 250 pounds, so I eat as close as I can to 250 grams of protein each day—about fifty grams per each of my five meals. If I'm busy and only have a chance to eat three meals, then I aim closer to eighty grams per meal that day. I don't overscrutinize this like some of my bodybuilder friends. I ballpark it—a big serving of eggs in the morning, a big chicken breast or two smaller chicken breasts for lunch—and that seems to work just fine. My female friends use the same tactic, but usually to weigh less. If they want to weigh 130 lbs, they multiply 130 by 0.75— because women's bodies are a little different—and eat ninety-five-ish grams of protein each day.

"I personally ignore headlines—or health gurus—offering me any advice on my diet. Regardless of what they're saying, I don't veer from the way I already eat. Gluten, for example, I don't give a shit about. Bread doesn't send me to the hospital, so I eat it when I eat it.

"I personally think vegans and vegetarians are SOL [shit out of luck]. A lot of my friends, and even some of my family, refuse to eat meat, but luckily, the ones I know were already naturally thin before they chose this lifestyle, because they've got plenty of other problems to deal with. Most vegs are very frail and prone to injury. They get sick more often and recover less quickly than us carnivores. And for whatever reason, they always seem to have horrible posture—I'm not sure of the correlation there, but it's pretty consistent." I noticed a handful of audience members suddenly pull their shoulders back and sit up straight in their seats.

"I personally eat shitty foods—pizza is possibly one of God's greatest inventions, Mexican food with salt-rimmed margaritas, sandwiches made with thick-ass slices of bread and cheese—but usually only once a week. If there's a special occasion or event, I might even eat this way two or more times in a week, and I don't sweat it because it's not the norm.

"I personally exercise. This is where my muscle comes from—not just from eating protein, like a lot of women fear—and the type of exercise I do also helps burn extra fat from my body, which is how I can be a little more relaxed than your average healthy eater when it comes to my pizza and beer."

It felt so great to be back up on the stage again—the bright lights on my face, my voice reverberating through the speaker system, the energy I felt coming from the audience.

The best part of that lecture was that I was being real again. I wasn't worried about convincing the audience of anything in particular; I was just alone onstage, sharing my thoughts. And what made it extra special was that I was spreading the right message. I was actually helping them, instead of just saying whatever they needed to hear in order for me to sell them my food.

"I'm going to keep it real: I was an asshole." The audience laughed even though I was being serious. "I made some horrible choices that probably affected many of you. And I want you to remember this, whether it was me or any other "expert" out there, the more we educate you on nutrition, the more you learn about your food, the less you truly know. I'm not talking about America's health problem right now; I'm talking to you." I waved my pointing finger through the audience. "Put on your blindfold—a blindfold to block all the marketing noise on TV, the advertising rhetoric in articles, the advice your doctor isn't qualified to give you, the nonsense on the food label—and I promise you you'll be smarter, eat better, and live healthier than you ever could without it.

"I'm Jeff Scot Philips, a recovering food industry asshole, and I thank you all for letting me share this with you today."

As they stood and cheered, I shoveled all of the food items off the two tables, leaving only the six selected items. On the left sat three boxes—one containing sugary bars, one containing processed potatoes, and one with brownies, all with labels and bolded buzz-words describing how healthy they allegedly were. On the right sat a label-less whole potato, an apple, and a bag of grapes. And to leave the audience with a lasting visual they wouldn't soon forget, I held up the blindfold before laying it on top of the food items, and then I left the stage.

EPILOGUE

NICOLE AND ALLEN

Two great friends of mine, Allen and Nicole, live together a few hours from me, in a town of fewer than 6,000 people, and since their household income is Allen's $17,000 a year salary, the closest place to buy groceries within their price range is Wal-Mart.

Nicole is overweight—about one hundred fifty pounds over-weight by her estimate—and had to apply for government assistance to help cover her ever-increasing medical bills. After every doctor visit she gets motivated to change her life and begins researching what she can do, on her budget, in her area. I've witnessed this woman take in the messages—"Blueberries are good for your health" and—"Protein is great for weight loss" and then run to Wal-Mart and pick up a case of protein bars with blueberries in them, and blue-berry protein smoothies. And after a month of eating and drinking nothing but those products, she can't understand why she's gained even more weight.

But then there's Allen, who shares the same town, bank account, and all of the same available information, and he's the most immac-ulate eater I know, with a six-pack and zero health issues. It drives Allen nuts that Nicole knows what he eats, has the same food avail-able to her, is encouraged and supported by him to eat it, and has extra motivation to eat healthy by the frustration of her personal body image and medical bills and issues.

One of them is the healthiest person I've ever met, while the other is at the polar opposite end of that spectrum.

Lack of knowledge is a problem, economic status is a problem, access to local quality food is a problem, but none of these things are *the* problem with America's obesity epidemic.

The problem is the profit-driven health and food industries that separate these two individuals. Some of us just happen to get lucky. For example, Allen and myself both happened to fall into the fitness component of the health and food industries from a young age. He and I don't have to exert willpower to avoid sweets or eat broccoli. Nicole, on the other hand, has the same problem with sweets that AA members have with alcohol, and the mere thought of broccoli makes her gag.

As a child she had fallen into the "Trix are for kids" component of these industries and grew accustomed to these types of foods, and as her biochemistry evolved over the next few decades, she grew addicted to them. By the time she reached adulthood and her metabolism slowed down, leaving her with excess weight that seemingly came out of nowhere, she was not only ill-equipped to make a change, her body and mind had been conditioned to be dependent on the very foods that harm her. She then turned to the weight-loss companies—owned by the same companies that created her addictions as a child—for a solution, and they know just what she wants: sweet and salty "health foods." The health and food industries kidnapped her, drugged her, and kept her until she developed the nutrition equivalent of Stockholm syndrome.

This isn't how an eating or malnutrition issue happens to everyone, of course. Some people don't eat enough food because they're busy. Add that to the stress of their job and you get increased cortisol, and possibly thyroid issues. Some of us have an uphill battle starting at birth thanks to our genetics. Some people, in certain areas, are on Electronic Benefit Transfers that won't allow them to buy the same healthy foods that you and I would eat, even if they want to. These are just a few of the examples of the sitting ducks with bull's-eyes on their backs, waiting for the food and weight-loss industries to prey upon. They get hit with marketing hidden under the guise of health articles, news segments, life-changing dietary fads, advertising, advice, services, and products purporting to help them, but all the while keeping them where they are, and in many cases making them worse.

As you've seen from my example, selling people shitty, harmful food isn't necessarily done on purpose—I'd actually like to believe it's never done on purpose—but because of the way the industry is put together, food companies are almost forced to do it. The magazines and news shows have to talk about something each day that satisfies the category of health, and since the way to eat healthy has been the same since forever, they've got to look for new angles to look at food and sexy dietary fads to talk about to keep you as a viewer or reader. This doesn't make them bad either; they're trying to do their job and give you information. The problem is, consumers take each new piece of information and run with it. When they do this, the food companies have to react if they want to stay relevant in the marketplace, and so they adjust their food to match consumer demands. Once their investors see that the new fad brings in money, then even if the food companies later realize that what they've done to their food is harmful (say, replacing the fat with sugar) the investors won't let them reverse it—at least not until the public trend switches, and consumers are OK with eating fat again, or whatever the next thing is.

If I've learned nothing else from my journey through the food and weight-loss industries, I've learned that everything is about distracting consumers. Even the health-food evangelists accidentally play into this. I believe Vani Hari, the Food Babe, wants to help as many people be healthy as possible, but in order to achieve this—in order to stop the food companies from harming people—she'll need to understand that when she poses two processed, unhealthy foods against each other, she helps us market those foods. When such a loved and trusted activist asks the question "Does your favorite candy have GMOs?" and pits Life Savers, for example, against Yummy Earth Organic Lollipops—which, as a side note, have almost twice as much sugar as Life Savers—and says to choose the latter because it's organic, the battle is already lost. All that argument does is justify to consumers that eating candy is OK as long as it doesn't have GMOs.

The foods needed for people to eat well and be healthy have always been the same. Those of us in the industry have never veered from them because we're keenly aware of, and often times creating, the distractions. The whole organic vs. GMOs argument is one of the biggest examples of this. The vast majority of fit and healthy people I know never focus on this. My friend Allen has never eaten anything organic in his life—he can't afford to—while Nicole on the other hand complains that since she can't afford organic potatoes, and since the healthy option is off the table for her, then, "Forget it. I might as well eat these baked potato chips instead—at least they're cheap, all natural, and gluten-free."

But this isn't about intentionally harming or deceiving consumers. It's not that any individual goes into the food industry thinking, "I'm going to manipulate the system in order to sell people foods packed with chemicals and get them sick." But because consumers have a food-purchasing thermostat in their heads—*the food must be above this quality, but below this price*—it's up to us companies to fight tooth and nail to fall into that range. This is just capitalism. It's competition. It's seeking an edge in an overcrowded marketplace. In order to survive—let alone thrive—those in the industry do whatever it takes to stay in business, get consumers' attention, and make them buy products.

When a company competes for distribution, shelf space, and consumer eyeballs in general, it has to address a ton of hidden elements. One of the first challenges I came across when I was in the game was that my food's taste needed to be craveable if you were going to buy it a second time. This is when the bad ingredients came into play, because people like the taste of sugar and fat, and if my competitors used it and consumers started buying their stuff over mine, I either had to adapt or go out of business.

Another important factor was that my margins needed to be high enough to appeal to my distributors and retailers, because I was essentially buying the right to sit on the top left side of people's screens or at the eye-level shelf at retail stores. Simultaneously, my retail price needed to be low, otherwise consumers would choose the cheaper, indistinguishable product next to mine. This is where the unpronounceable ingredients start creeping in, because they're processed and often synthetic, and subsidized by the government, which means they're cheaper. Earlier I mentioned Monsanto infiltrating the FDA, one reason being so it could pass, and/or keep in place, the legislation that gave tax dollars back to itself to produce its nonorganic food. And, of course, when the government is covering Monsanto's business costs, it can afford to charge manufacturers like myself way less for its products than the organic farmer up the road. This puts me between a P&L sheet and a hard place.

Next, assuming I'd get prime-time eyeball real estate, I had to worry about my message. If my marketing and packaging didn't contain all the appealing buzzwords and snazzy narrative, customers wouldn't have ever thought to reach for my products. My competitor said paleo, gluten-free, low-calorie, and organic, so then I had to say it too. It's an interesting dynamic when you're simultaneously in charge and at the behest of a market that demands impossible things. We circle round around the consumers' demands, all the while harming them in the process. And in the food industry this is the CEO's dilemma.

My friend Walt has been a car salesman for as long as I've known him, and we've had numerous discussions about this subject. He often questions the sales tactics that he's trained to use on customers, but his reasoning always returns to, What am I supposed to do when I know customers' incomes inevitably make their monthly payments a stretch, but they're dead set on purchasing that shiny new muscle car anyway? Should he refuse to sell them the car they want? "That wouldn't change anything for them," he justifies, "because they'll just go across the street and buy the same car from my competitor.

Besides, if I don't sell a car soon," he further defends his ethics, "how am I supposed to feed my family that month?" In other words, the question is not, should Walt sell the customer the overpriced muscle car? The only relevant question is, who gets to profit *when* the customer buys that overpriced muscle car?

And that's the same question I had to ask myself. *When* consumers buy their cheap, tasty food with the misleading health claims, who gets to make the sale: James Chambers at Weight Watchers, Monty Sharma at Jenny Craig, Dawn Zier at NutriSystem, or me?

I learned about manipulation from the biggest food retailers in the world, I learned about spreading diet fads from the media, I learned how important the "wealth above health" philosophy is from investors, I learned about food label deception from the government agencies like the USDA. But one element that I think often goes overlooked—when trying to solve America's obesity, and health-care, epidemics—is the consumers. At the end of the day, consumers drive all of the food and weight-loss industries' efforts—because they're the ones spending the money that the companies are after. They initiate the demand, and then get harmed as all the moving parts of the food and weight-loss industries work together to supply it.

Two people, Nicole and Allen—for one of thousands, if not millions of examples—share the same bank account, available grocery options, and constant marketing in their face. One's lean and healthy; the other is not. And for the same reason that America struggles with gun violence, we struggle with obesity, diabetes, and heart disease: because the ones most susceptible to falling victim to it are the ones fighting so desperately to keep it. It's the least healthy of us who spend the most time reading food labels. It's the least healthy of us who don't understand that how we vote for our political leaders affects our food system, and our medical bills. It's the least healthy of us who put the most effort into eating healthy, sadly, and who fund the health-food industry's growth. And it's for this reason that the solution is *not* to try to convince the average consumer to make smarter, healthier purchasing choices.

Possibly the most important thing I learned from studying McDonald's was that any problem is never a human problem; it's a systems problem, and anything and everything within a system can be fixed by tweaking the system. We need a change to our political system—if the 2016 presidential campaign hasn't proven this, I don't know what will—so that food companies, pharmaceutical companies, etc., can't buy their way into the FDA and USDA. We need a change in our media, and the way information gets disseminated out to the public, so that consumers don't keep getting tricked into ridiculous diet fads and myths. And most important—for fuck's sake—we need a change to our financial system, so that food company CEOs, like I used to be, aren't able to, and aren't pressured to, degrade their ingredients, manipulate their nutrition labels and marketing, and deceive consumers into paying for food that's making them sick.

ACKNOWLEDGMENTS

First, thanks to Joel Gotler for taking a chance on me, and to my literary agent, Murray Weiss, for all of your guidance during this process.

Huge thanks to everyone at Regan Arts for all the great work you've done (FYI: To all of you who asked me, "Is it safe to be eating this?" If you have to ask then the answer's *no!*) And an extra special thanks to my editor, Alexis Gargagliano, for putting up with my colorful language and somehow converting my graphic stories into an actual book. You are some kind of magician!

Adam Lester, and Mandy and Adam Chase, thanks for continually inspiring me throughout the writing process. You know what all you've meant to me; there's no need to boost your egos anymore than that. Thanks to my mother, and favorite success story, for playing a lead supporting role in *all* of this—especially after that time I tricked you into accompanying me on live TV.

And thanks to Dave (the one from the story) for talking with me, just about every day, to help keep my drinking under control during the writing process, and thanks to my pop, Mr. Bill, for supplying much of the wine I consumed after getting off the phone with Dave.

ABOUT THE AUTHOR

Jeff Scot Philips is a nutritionist, professional speaker, and entrepreneur. He founded Break The Cycle Inc, a seminar hosting company, before creating Fit Food, which later became Lean Eats, and then Fit Chefs. He now spends most of his time speaking about the corruption in the food and weight-loss industries, and teaching consumers what they can do to avoid falling victim to it.

If you'd like to hear Jeff's take on the latest food trends and to hear him expose the current misleading health information, join his mailing list at www.bigfatfoodfraud.com.